A HEALTHY DIVORCE

Divorce Program Correspondence Course

Includes

Parenting Plan with Videos

and

How To Self-Mediate Your Entire Divorce

NATIONALLY APPROVED

Parent and Family Stabilization Course/Divorce Program

or

Court Ordered By Judicial Circuit Court

Authored By Debbie Shooter,

Off Campus Education and Publishing

CAPITOL HILL

611 PENNSYLVANIA AVE. S.E. STE.258

WASHINGTON, DC20003-4303

Contact: 1-800-853-1148 or 1-407-324-2400

FOR ANY QUESTIONS ABOUT THIS PROGRAM GO TO:

questions@divorceprogram.com

Nationally this program is recognized as an exceptional program regarding Divorce. It covers all states time in class requirements, security questions, and quality of program. However the following states and only these states as yet do not accept any online programs. However they might in some circumstance accepts a correspondence course. These states are Delaware, Minnesota, Utah, Virginia, West Virginia, and Connecticut. If you live in these states check to see if they will give you a waiver to take our correspondence course. If you do not live in these states, most likely this program is right for you.

Less than 1/2 of 1% of judges nationally do not accept the Divorce program online, but most because of persons not being able to leave their home, find a babysitter, or live a far distance from a school will accept a correspondence course. Nationally all states including the above accept our Co-Parenting program for its exceptional Divorce Plan and Mediation Plan which is a part of your Co-Parenting Program.

If you need a great program to help you get through your divorce or you get a waiver to take a correspondence course or online course from the ½ to 1% of judges that do not like online programs/correspondence courses (but usually makes an exception), this is the best program by far (and judges will agree) out there for the information you need in acquiring a divorce.

Table of Contents

Copyright Notice	Page 1
Introduction	Page 3
Forward	Page 9
Let's Examine Your Divorce	Page 13
The Grieving Process	Page 17
How Co-Parenting Is Similar To Working With Co-Workers	Page 27
How Do Children Learn	Page 29
Planning A Healthy Separation For The Children	Page 33
Dealing With Clothes And Personal Articles	Page 43
Negotiate Financial Responsibilities During The Separation And Importance Of Play	Page 45
Decide How Much Time You And Your Spouse/Partner Want To Spend With Each Other	Page 55
Child(ren) Need Honesty And Information During The Divorce Process	Page 57
The Decision To Divorce	Page 59
Developing A Parenting Plan	Page 73
From Adolescents To Becoming A Teenager	Page 97
I.R.S. Tax Credit	Page 101
Transporting Children, Costs Of Schools, Who Pays, Who Chooses School? Spouse And Sharing Children.	Page 105

How Do You Stay Connected With Your Spouse/Partner When You Have The Children? Children Need To Know Their Grandparents.	Page 109
Traveling Out Of State Or Country?	Page 111
After Divorce, When Family Still Counts.	Page 113
Child Support Guidelines/Child Support Amounts	Page 117
Health And Dental Care For Children: Insurance And Sharing Costs Not Covered By Insurance.	Page 119
Handling Religious Education, How Do Courts Decide Which Religion The Child(ren) Should Follow When Parents Of Different Religions Separate?	Page 121
Yearly Access Plan	Page 131
Financial And Property Issues	Page 135
Reminders To Help You Help Your Child(ren) After The Divorce	Page 139
Explore Where You Are, And Where You Are Going After Divorce.	Page 141
Discover A New Life Within; Setting Long And Short Term Goals	Page 145
Spousal Abuse, Verbal Abuse, Sexual Abuse, And Physical Abuse	Page 149
A Discussion Regarding When Parents Kidnap	Page 157
National and Local Resources for Inquiries and Help Line	Page 159
Going Pro Se	Page 163
Test Questions	Page 165

Copyright Notice

Typography: New Times Roman; First Edition, 2002, v. 1.0, REVISED 2014

Copyright information and references available upon request.

Divorce Advisor and Mediator: Deborah Shooter

Editor: William Shooter

Prepared for publication By: Jon Watters

Publisher's Cataloging-in-Publication: Shooter, Deborah A.

"A HEALTHY DIVORCE" Everyone directly involved with a divorce will respond differently to their own experience.

NOTICE OF PUBLISHING RIGHTS AND COPYRIGHTS

"A HEALTHY DIVORCE AGREEMENT"

A PROGRAM REGARDING SEPARATION AND DIVORCE USING VIDEO'S AND INCLUDED WORKBOOK WILL BE SOLD SUBJECT TO THE CONDITION AND USE AS AGREED.

That it shall not, by way of trade or otherwise, be lent, resold, hired out, or otherwise circulated without the publisher's prior written consent. This program may not be reproduced in any form of binding or cover other than that in which it is published and without a similar condition including this condition being imposed on the subsequent purchase. The program is entirely whole. No part of the book can be separated and used in conjunction or with other material that could relate to other programs. The scanning, uploading, and distribution of this book via the internet or by any other means without written permission of the publisher is illegal and punishable by law.

ASK YOUR STATE IF YOU ARE ALLOWED TO TAKE YOUR DIVORCE PROGRAM AND PARENTING PLAN THROUGH A PRIVATE INSTRUCTOR AND CORRESPONDENCE COURSE?

Please purchase only authorized electronic/original programs (not copies) editions, and do not participate in or encourage electronic piracy of copyrighted material. Your support of the author's rights is appreciated.

The book, workbook and chapter videos that are incorporated in "A HEALTHY DIVORCE" includes copyrights from four different sources.

"A HEALTHY DIVORCE" has been granted permission through licensing agreements or written permission to produce for them a DVD video for classroom and education purpose only. If you have purchased the program or received a certificate by taking the program "A HEALTHY DIVORCE" you have permission to watch the videos as they are part of the program.

NOTICE OF COPYRIGHT © FROM ALL FOUR PUBLISHING GROUPS. ALL RIGHTS RESERVED.

Video used in this course are from the program Crossroads of Parenting and Divorce (Copyright © by Susan Boyan and Anne Marie Termini) and used with permission of the publisher, Active Parenting Publishers, Inc. of Marietta GA. No part of this program may be reproduced without prior written permission of the publisher.

Chapters of Video published by Active Parenting Publishers, Inc. consists of Chapter Video 3-11 and 13-21. Deborah Shooter, Off Campus Education and Publishing produced Chapter Video 1, 2, and 12 (Copyright © 2010 Video), Images Copyright © 2002, 2011, 2013, 2014, 2015 I stock and their affiliates produced photos. All rights reserve.

All Copyright © Notice and Verification upon written request.

Introduction

OFFICE HOURS

Our office is open Monday thru Friday 9:00 A.M. to 5:00 P.M. Eastern Time.

Our Privacy Policy, Refund Policy, and Security Policy can be emailed to your computer during normal business hours. Please request in writing what policy you require and we will provide it to you through your computer.

- ✓ **Welcome,** this program was designed to make your experience a pleasant one. You simply read the material, fill in the workbook, get to know our curriculum including videos. Please pay attention to the information that has a check mark in front of it.

If you are taking this class on your own or if the state you filed your divorce in does not require you to take a timed class, please disregard this section.

Depending on the state you filed your divorce in, please follow their guide lines to how much time you are required to spend in class. Each state has different time requirements to follow when studying the program/class.

You can take as long as 60 days to finish the program.

We ask that you come prepared. You will need several sheets of paper to write on, a pen, and if you have a journal, this would be a good time to write down your thoughts and ideas.

Sometimes you will be asked questions. The Parenting Plan and workbook is a big part of your program. It is required that you participate and complete all written parts of the course including #1 Guide to Writing a Parenting Plan".

Will there be a test?

NO! Unless the state you filed your divorce in requires it. We have provided a test for you to take if necessary or if you want to test your skills to see how well you did with this course. WE DO NOT REQUIRE AN EXAM OR TEST TO GET A CERTIFICATE. Some states like Maryland do require an exam. After you finish the exam, please contact us at 407-324-2400 to allow us to grade your exam.

WHEN YOU SIGN UP FOR AN "APPROVED" CORRESPONDENCE COURSE, WHAT DOES THE STATE YOU FILED YOUR DIVORCE IN REQUIRE FROM YOU?

✓ *Security Questions*

The state you are getting your divorce from requires some type of security feature in each program given, to make sure the person who takes a course (not in a classroom or proctored environment) is the same person that signed up for the course.

We believe that if you are reading the material and answering the Security Word Question, writing down what page you found the security word on, most likely it will take you the four, six, twelve, or sixteen hours that your state court is requiring you to be in the course; to finish it. We cannot predict the time a very fast reader would start and finish this course. This course is based on an adult average reader. We ask you to read the course and do the workbook, for as long as your state requires. When we send you a program, that program will take the minimum amount of time, to finish the program based on your state requirements. All we ask is that you begin and read, do the workbook and stay the course until you have completed the entire program. If you have done that we are confident; you will participate in the required amount of time your state requires.

SECURITY WORD QUESTIONS, BE READY FOR THEM.

You will be asked to answer Security Word Questions. Once you start the course, a Security Word Question may be found in the section you are reading. If that happens, answer the question on the Security Requirements Sheet we have provided you and go on with your program. What you will see is this; Security Word One Question is: custody. You would write in your Security Requirement Sheet on the appropriate line One/custody. It is that simple. Once you are finished with the program, you may call us or fax/mail your Security Requirement Sheet. Once we receive the sheet, we will send you your certificate.

If you are calling in your security word answers call: 407-324-2400
If you are faxing in your security word answers call: 410-645-8512
If you are mailing in your security word answers write to:

Divorce Program
CAPITOL HILL
611 PENNSYLVANIA AVE. S.E. STE.258
WASHINGTON, DC 20003-4303

KEEP TRACK OF YOUR TIME SPENT IN THE PROGRAM.

You need to be aware that we have two security conditions. The second requirement is *All students of the Parent Education and Family Stabilization Course must remain within the course and its content for the minimum time required.* You also are required to keep track of the time you are in the course. The state you filed your divorce in requires you to take a course that is 4,6,12, or 16 hours long. When you sign in, the clock starts ticking. When you sign out, the clock stops. Your state wants you to keep track of the time you are in the course. We have sent you a Security Requirements Sheet. Please when you start reading your program, write in the date and time you started the program in the appropriate line. When you sign out, please do the same thing. Keep track of the time you are in the program.

When you finish the program, you will be asked to certify that you are the one who took the course and that what you wrote regarding the time you spent in the course is correct. You will sign that what you wrote was true and correct. You do not have to read the entire program in one sitting. You have 60 days to complete the program.

Your instructors are here to help you. Call 407-324-2400, your instructor is waiting for your call.

The components of the Parent Education and Family Stabilization Course are intended for educational purposes only. Any instructor, who gives advice in this program, only will relate to the subject matter within the guidelines of the program. It is understood that we cannot give mental health advice or provide therapy, medicine or treat any disorder. In the event you have a question regarding mental health disorders we strongly suggest you contact a mental health counselor or doctor. We encourage you to seek on-going assistance through a licensed medical facility or mental health center. We are not attorneys and cannot give legal advice.

A Healthy Divorce is "NATIONALLY" recognized in most jurisdictions where they allow access to classroom correspondence/online programs with instructor assistance. Our Parenting classes are widely recognized by county courts; however, if you are court ordered to take a parent education class, we honor your judge's decision to accept our class or not. It is always best to check with your county court, government agency or designated administrator in your area to verify their acceptance of an online / correspondence program. This course meets and exceeds the Family Stabilization/Parent

Education requirements. If you are taking this course to fulfill a state court or legal requirement, please make sure you explain to your judge/attorney that not only are you taking a virtual course, our course includes instructors to guide you through your program, as well as help you sort out and give assistance writing your parenting plan. The book when delivered is considered used; therefor "A Healthy Divorce" will not issue a refund for this program. "A Healthy Divorce is not responsible for any client-side technical problem with DVD or student not understanding how to operate a DVD.

Certificate; sent to you as soon as you finish course.

Completing this course, "A Healthy Divorce" will provide an original "certified" certificate of course completion to the parent/caregiver. We also make available when requested "certified" originals to your attorney, judge, caseworker, probation officer, counselor, or any other person you deemed should have an original "certified" course completion certificate. You may make copies as well for these individuals. However you are responsible for providing a copy not an original "certified" to the above. Your privacy is important to us. Only persons you request we send original certificates to will get a certificate. Please call us and we will send you your certificate by the next business day. 407-324-2400

How do you want your certificate sent?

If you are calling in call: 407-324-2400

If you are faxing in your security word information, add where you want the certificate to be sent: 410-645-8512

If you are mailing in your security word answers write to the below address and send where you want us to send certificate:

Divorce Program

CAPITOL HILL

611 PENNSYLVANIA AVE. S.E. STE.258

WASHINGTON, DC 20003-4303

A Healthy Divorce - Required information needed by most states (family and children agencies) if you want a certificate issued for taking this program.

SECURITY WORD QUESTIONS

When you start the program, watch for sentence "Security word "WORD-TO-NOTE" note word and page number." When you see this sentence write the "WORD-TO-NOTE" and the page number you found it on in the table below. You will find 10 security questions. Thank you.

	WORD-TO-NOTE	page #		WORD-TO-NOTE	page #
#1			#6		
#2			#7		
#3			#8		
#4			#9		
#5			#10		

TIME SPEND IN YOUR PROGRAM

Each time you work in the Divorce Program, just enter the time you started the program and finished the program as well. During the current session, add up the total time you worked in the program (Hours and Minutes).

Date: _____ Start Time: _____ Finish Time: _____ Total Time in Program: _____
Date: _____ Start Time: _____ Finish Time: _____ Total Time in Program: _____
Date: _____ Start Time: _____ Finish Time: _____ Total Time in Program: _____
Date: _____ Start Time: _____ Finish Time: _____ Total Time in Program: _____
Date: _____ Start Time: _____ Finish Time: _____ Total Time in Program: _____
Date: _____ Start Time: _____ Finish Time: _____ Total Time in Program: _____
Date: _____ Start Time: _____ Finish Time: _____ Total Time in Program: _____
Date: _____ Start Time: _____ Finish Time: _____ Total Time in Program: _____
Date: _____ Start Time: _____ Finish Time: _____ Total Time in Program: _____
Date: _____ Start Time: _____ Finish Time: _____ Total Time in Program: _____
Date: _____ Start Time: _____ Finish Time: _____ Total Time in Program: _____
Date: _____ Start Time: _____ Finish Time: _____ Total Time in Program: _____
Date: _____ Start Time: _____ Finish Time: _____ Total Time in Program: _____

CERTIFICATE PROGRAM VERIFICATION OF COMPLETION

This is to verify that I (YOUR NAME) _____ completed the Divorce Program and spent the required time the State of (ADD STATE WHERE YOU FILED YOUR DIVORCE) _____ required of me to spend learning divorce procedures and Co-Parenting techniques.

Signed: _____ Date: _____

FORWARD

INTRODUCTION LETTER FROM AUTHOR OF "A HEALTHY DIVORCE", DEBORAH SHOOTER

Welcome to "A Healthy Divorce". We are so happy that you have joined us.

The student does not have to worry about if they answered the Questions in workbook correctly; for the most part there is no right or wrong answer. There are many ways a situation can be viewed. Equally, there are many ways to plan your Parenting Plan. Example: how are you going to arrange an activity, vacation, with your child(ren) or how to come up with answers to save for your child(ren)'s college education? Look at all of your options (be creative, think outside the box) and then come up with answers that appear to work best for your individual family.

Similarly, individuals when in disagreement sometimes come up with two totally different ideas. Look at each idea, and weight each answer. Is it an issue that you really need to counter? Even if the other parent's concept is different than yours, the end result may work out fine.

Without finding fault, try to work through your ex's ideas/requests, without always saying "no". You may consider giving a little on certain topics that relate to what you are already thinking and agree to.

Additionally, give your spouse/partner choices when there are two or more options that you have already found acceptable. Example: The student says to their spouse/partner, "I would like the child(ren) to spend two weeks next summer vacationing with me in Alaska the first two weeks in June or the first two weeks in July." Then let your spouse/partner choose what works best for him/her.

Learn to save your battles for negotiations where there is little compromise or when both parents are in total disagreement.

Before we get started, it is important for you to know that this program is not going to intrude in your lives, question your parenting skills, or tell you how to raise your child(ren). Let's face it at times we have all failed at being the perfect mom or dad. Most likely both you and your partner have made parenting mistakes; however the program "A Healthy Divorce" does not address your parenting skills or lack of. On the contrary, as a co-parent we want to celebrate your new life. That is our only goal.

As educators we will share ideas on how to understand the process of becoming co-parents/co-partners. Unless you have a degree in social work, most likely it is hard to understand the concept of shared or co-parenting. For most, in the past, as a couple you worked together, shared ideas and concerns as you raised your child(ren) together.

The circumstances now have changed. No longer do you have shared interests except most likely when it comes to your child(ren). For most, divorce is taken very seriously. It would be unusual if feelings of fear did not take hold. Shortly after parents start thinking the "D" word, they also start concerning themselves about losing control of their child(ren). For most parents that does not have to happen. Your child(ren) loves both of you. That will never change. New people, new interests will come into your child's life; however what will never change is the love your child(ren) have for you. Knowing that, from here on out, until one of you die, you and your partner are going to form a co-parenting role. You can form a solid partnership, or you can fail appallingly. However it is certain, good or bad, you will, become a co-parent after separation. Working together for the betterment of the child(ren) supports their development by giving them better access to both parents. Equal rights and shared parenting, does not always mean that both parents get access to their child(ren) 50% (equally) all of the time. It does mean that both parents work together to provide the best access to their child(ren); resulting in each parent receiving quality time.

Everything is not always equal, but at the end of the day, both parents should feel that their concerns regarding development of their child(ren) are being met, and best of all the kids are living and having a quality relationship with both parents. It is important that both parents have adequate visitation, paying their share of child support, and have a say about how the child(ren) are being raised. Co-Parenting for most gives both parents a shared partnership as they settle into a workable, yet different role. This relationship goes from working together as a married or equal partnership to going full circle as separate individuals. Each developing a relationship of understanding and hopefully acceptance while working towards a final goal as co-parents; forming a divorce and separate lasting relationship. The word "lasting" is the key.

Look at the best way to give equal access to both parents. Remember, work schedules and school conflicts have to be taken into account. Sometimes parents will not have equal access to their child(ren). Sometimes work schedules conflict. Parents might have to ask themselves, what is more important, the job, school, or the kids?

These decisions are not easy. A parent that has a great paying job sometimes cannot just walk away, because they are the sole income provider. Another parent going to school might be badgered by the other partner, because they are not bringing any income in. Usually there is a shining light at most ends of the tunnel. Once the parent getting their education, graduates, the immediate stress will dissipate when that parent is now able to provide income for themselves and the family.

The following story is called: **"THE MISGUIDED HOUSEHOLD"** The wife took this class and during class she told her classmates her husband works at home. Her story is an example showing how co-parenting may or may not work. In this case the mother/wife wanted it entirely her way. The wife is on the road selling widgets all week long. The wife demands that the couple's five children live with her in her brand new four bedroom apartment as well as the children must go to the school one block from her home. When she is out-of-town she will provide care for the children by hiring a nanny.

She will be asking the court to require the husband to pay the salary for the nanny as she needs someone to stay with the children, during the time she is working and away from the household. On weekends the husband (who lives in the same town, close to the children's school) can have the kids as long as the children go to the husband's parent's home to spend the night. Since the husband is living with his parents, that would work out well.

Think about the best solution that you would make for this family's living situation. I hope that you looked at the above situation and found that everything should be reversed.

If the mother is going to be out of town and the father works out of his home, the best place for the children would be at dad's home during the week. This way a stranger would not be watching the children, a costly nanny would not have to be hired, grandparents would be around to help dad out and mom would have the kids on the weekends. Leaving it the way it was, mom would never see the children.

Sometimes a little common sense goes a long way. Sometimes common sense goes out the window when people are hurt or scared. Co-parenting does work. Even so, like anything else regarding relationships, you have to work hard to maintain a quality divorce or separation connection.

We look forward to getting your feedback. Thank you again for choosing our program. We appreciate your business. If there is anything we can do, to help you get more out of our program please do not hesitate to ask. Again our phone number is 1-800-853-1148.

Sincerely Yours,
Deborah Shooter

Chapter 1 - A Healthy Divorce - Let's Examine Your Divorce

WORKBOOK QUESTIONS,

(1-1) Months or years of unhappiness? _____

Clouds of Doubt

Some habits that you have observed changing; maybe you are the one changing. Check if you see you or your partner changing. Then fill in the blanks for the rest of this section in the workbook.

Habits that changed/are changing:

(1-2) Spending more money on self?

_____ Yourself _____ Spouse

(1-3) Pushing spouse's buttons to provoke confrontation?

_____ Yourself _____ Spouse

(1-4) Going back to school, new job?

_____ Yourself _____ Spouse

(1-5) Going out evenings, spending time with friends without spouse?

_____ Yourself _____ Spouse

(1-6) Other activities that never happened prior or things that your spouse or you have done that were totally out of character to how they/you lived in the past?

_____ Yourself _____ Spouse

(1-7) Why do you believe you or your spouse have come to this point in your marriage where you admit that you/your spouse/or both are unhappy in your marriage?

_____

_____

(1-8) Are you the one that left or the one that was left behind?

_____

Date: _____ Comment, (How are you doing?)

_____

_____

Have you had FANTASIES LIKE?

Getting on a plane and just leaving?

Pursuing an old high school sweet heart you've often fantasized about?

Being swept off your feet and carried away by a perfect lover?

Imagined your spouse being killed suddenly in an automobile accident?

Other fantasies; different from your normal thought patterns?

If you have had fantasies such as the above, you are very normal. Most people do not act on their fantasies, however some do. Realize for the most part they are just fantasies; a safe place to go where you may relieve stress, to find hope, to dream, and to find temporary peace.

Even thoughts where you wish your spouse harm are normal. You are looking for ways to release the pain, the hurt, the damage that the other person has caused you. You just want to find resolution. Sometimes it takes months, even years, to get your life back to what you saw as normal. Sometimes what was once normal will never exist again. However, the new normal might just be a better place and a little more tolerable.

Time will change circumstances. Usually we find time will make us stronger. There is a lot of change going on in your life right now, no doubt about it. During this time period if you need help, need a person to talk to just pick up the phone. Look in the back of this program for resources and make that phone call. There are professional people and organizations out there that are waiting by the phone for people in crisis to call them. They are there to help you. Please ask for help.

We all are human; we survive in good times and bad. From time to time, especially in bad times, we all could use a little help.

Please answer the next set of questions.

(1-9) Did you stay together for the sake of child(ren)?

_____
_____
_____

(1-10) How are the child(ren) doing through all of the change?

_____
_____
_____

(1-11) What are you doing to help get them through this period of adjustment?

_____
_____
_____

(1-12) What is your spouse/partner doing (to help your child(ren), and to help you to get through this same period of adjustment?

_____
_____
_____

(1-13) Do you see yourself going in the right direction? Please explain.

_____
_____
_____

A Healthy Divorce

(1-14) Planning a healthy separation for the child(ren). Understand the place you are at, so you may find the right steps to move forward. Where are you heading?

_____

_____

Reconciliation: _____

Second Thoughts: _____

Separation: _____

Divorce: _____

Are you a single Parent? Single Parent (Moving on): _____

(1-15) What are some of the emotions that you have been feeling lately concerning your separation and divorce? Check off each word that describes the way you are feeling.

Confusion _____

Disappointment _____

Frustration _____

Anger _____

Rage _____

Sadness _____

Embarrassment _____

Loneliness _____

Hurt _____

Regret _____

Jealousy _____

Other _____

NOTES:

Chapter 2 - A Healthy Divorce - The Grieving Process

Some people learn about grieving when they or their spouse or partner leave their marriage or have left the relationship. If you feel like you are grieving, this is normal. It is healthy to go through a grieving (mourning) process when going through a separation/divorce.

When you complete the agonizing processes, you will be in a better place to move on. Without grieving some people will be stuck in a place called yesterday, living with your memory of hurt, inconsolable despair, and sometimes even hatred. Security word divorce note word and page number. Most will describe it as being broken hearted, grief-stricken, or feeling devastated. You will (as for most people) learn to trust your feelings again; feel good about yourself; even feel good about new relationships. It takes time.

Let's look at a soon-to-be divorcee named Susan. She stated, "When each of my two sisters divorced, my mother made the same comment regarding their divorce." Mom said, "Divorce is like a death in the family. Holiday gatherings are no longer the same, the dynamic has shifted, and in a lot of ways the control over your life, my children's life has shifted." Susan continues, "I always wanted to make sure my children were always protected. The control I had over my family is gone or somewhat altered, yet I must conform, I must go on." Susan and her family show us they had a difficult time adapting to the grieving process.

What Susan and her family experienced is painful and sadly normal for a lot of people. Human beings are designed for relationships, whether it is that of a friend, lover, parent, or child(ren). When those relationships end, the deep roots are not cast aside with the signing of a court document. It often takes months or even years to truly move on.

LET'S LOOK AT SOME OF THE PHASES YOU EXPERIENCE WHILE GOING THROUGH THE DIVORCE PROCESS.

- Denial
- Anger
- Shock
- Rollercoaster
- Bargaining
- Depression
- Numbness/Disorganization (If applicable)
- Letting Go
- Acceptance

EMOTIONAL STAGES ONE GOES THROUGH DURING DIVORCE

Everyone will react differently to divorce. There are common stages you will go through. If you have experienced a death of a loved one, you most likely have experienced stages of grief that you can associate with. Knowing what to expect will help you find your way through the difficult stages; yet preparing and educating yourself about divorce still does not take the pain and heartbreak away. DIVORCE HURTS!

It is common for people to be stuck for a long period of time in one stage of grief during a separation or divorce. Some people find they re-visit stages as they move back and forth working their way through the grief process. You may find some of the stages easier to navigate than others. The thing to remember is that you eventually will make your way through to healing and hope.

Denial:

You find it hard to believe this is happening to you. You refuse to accept that the relationship is over and struggle with trying to find solutions to the marital problems. You will spend time believing that if you do or say the right thing your spouse will come home. Perhaps you hate feeling out of control some-what regarding your own destiny, as well as the destiny of your marriage. You will be convinced that divorce is not the solution to the marital problems. For hours you may sit, looking out the window, wondering if your spouse will drive by. Surely he/she is worried about the family? You could have bouts of crying, some even experience wailing, sobbing, coming from your deepest spirit, a place where there is no consoling; utter despair or disbelief.

You will tell yourself stories to try to make sense of it and your imagination will run wild. You will wonder if there was more you could have done, or if there is anything wrong with you. Maybe your spouse never even loved you. You will wonder if your entire marriage was a lie.

There is a lot of mental re-hashing during this period. You will feel as if you can't control your thinking and find yourself obsessed with the failure of your marriage. Depression is a danger you might have to contend with at this stage as you may find yourself crying at the drop of a hat.

Anger/Shock:

You will feel panic, rage, and numbness or feel like you are going crazy. You will swing between despair that your marriage is over and hope that it will be restored. It will seem impossible to cope with these feelings. You will experience some common fears when thinking about your future alone. You will wonder how you are going to survive your divorce. Will you ever find love again, will the pain ever end or will you feel this way the rest of your life?

Rollercoaster:

You can't seem to settle your feelings and thoughts. You swing from being hopeful to feelings of utter despair. During this stage, you will try to intellectualize what has happened. If you can only understand what is going on the pain will go away and all will make sense again.

Bargaining:

You are still holding onto the hope that your marriage will be restored. There is a willingness to change anything about yourself. You are willing to do anything; if you could just get it right, your spouse would return. The important thing to learn during this stage is that you can't control the thoughts, desires or actions of another human being.

Depression:

When you look at yourself as the rock in the family, and you start seeing your rock is crumbling into pieces; you could find the pieces are hard to put back into place. Depression is a serious medical condition that can take so much out of you. It can make you feel like you do not want to even get out of bed, or that it is hard to just get through the day. Depression can make you feel sad, helpless, and uninterested in your favorite activities.

Depression is different than feeling sad or blue. Feelings of sadness go away with time, whereas depression can last for weeks, months, or even years. Depression is not your fault. It's not a personal weakness or a condition that you can just "snap out of" and feel better. Depression is a common condition. An estimated 35 million U.S. adults have experienced depression at some point. Most likely in your case, you are depressed because of the circumstances surrounding your separation and/or divorce. There is help for depression. People get relief from their symptoms each and every day. It starts by making a phone call to your primary doctor or the health clinic you attend. Start today, you will feel better as soon as you reach out for help.

Numbness/Disorganization:
These feelings allow your body to emotionally shut down. Most people look at it as a time where you cannot get it together, a time of confusion, a time where you cannot manage your life, career, or even organize daily functions. Many people when going through a loss find it difficult to explain, however here are some of the explanations I have heard to denote numbness/disorganization. Harry described it as a failure to be able to breathe. James said he would lie in bed and stare at the ceiling. Some people tried to get rid of the numbness, by trying to find someone to hold on to, rebound with another person to cover up the pain. Tina dwelled on what would never be, blamed herself for the breakup. George just described it as being in shock, an insulation to protect you from more damage, emotional or otherwise. Robert, who has raced cars over in Daytona described it this way, "Relationships are like driving. You can be the best in the world but that doesn't mean someone else won't mess it up. Someone else can crash right into you!"

Letting Go:

> Emotionally you realize that your marriage is over. There is nothing you can do or say to change the inevitable. You will become more willing to forgive the faults of your spouse/partner and take responsibility for your part in the breakdown of the marriage. You will begin to feel a sense of liberation and some hope for the future.

Acceptance:

> The obsessive thoughts have stopped; the need to heal your marriage is behind you. You begin to feel as if you can and will have a fulfilling life. Suddenly you are looking ahead and not behind you, you are making plans and following through with them. You will open up to the idea of finding new interests. This is a period of growth where you will discover that you have strengths and talents and are able to go forward in spite of the fear you feel. Your pain gives way to hope and you discover that there is life after divorce and the future is made brighter due to the pain you have suffered.

While these phases are usually associated with death, they can hold just as true for divorce. Grief and grieving are processes that each human being experiences and not only in the death of a loved one. We grieve for lost love, for what could or should have been. We grieve for the loss of a family dynamic, a familiar family unit. The parting that takes place in divorce can often times be as final as death.

You may be surprised by the long, arduous journey of emotions that you are experiencing, the seemingly insurmountable mountains and endless valleys.

There is no right or wrong way to work through your individual emotional phases. Being aware that they are there and giving them validation, often times will move you farther along your unique path of grief. Be prepared for unexpected reoccurrences in the future, months or even years after you believed that you were through with it, and had moved beyond the reach of the pain.

These flashback events are most often triggered by important life events; such as the graduation or marriage of a child, moving from a home with strong emotional ties, the birth of a child(ren) or grandchild(ren), or the death of a loved one. It is generally believed that our painful memories are all stored in the same part of the brain, so a new emotional experience can open the floodgates to old memories and the accompanying pain of grief and loss. We can be taken completely by surprise, as the agonizing memories come crashing back like massive emotional tsunamis.

By expecting these occasional relapses and remembering that there is not a completion date to grief, you allow your emotions to flow through the stages at their individual pace. Also, realize that you may revisit a phase you thought you were finished with many times, and that is okay. Your mind knows what it needs and will process the information continually until it reaches some level of acceptance, allowing you to move beyond the grief while turning towards the first page of your new chapter of life.

Allow yourself validation for your pain and grief and distance yourself from those who undermine your progress. You are a unique person and your suffering, coping, and determination to move forward will enable you to find new skills as individual as you are. Simply said "that is the way we were made."
Life is a journey, not a destination; we move forward one step at a time.

WORKBOOK QUESTIONS,

(2-1) What stage of life are you in when we address the "grieving process"?

_____

_____

_____

(2.2) Are you or have you experienced some or all of these situations?

_____

_____

_____

(2-3) Today, the hardship for you is:

_____

_____

_____

2-4) Hardship for my spouse/partner:

_____

_____

_____

(2-5) Hardship for my child(ren):

(2-6) Hardship for your family, parents, friends, co-workers etc.:

(2-7) Besides being required to take this class; what would you like to get out of this program today?

Notes:

Chapter 3 - A Healthy Divorce - How Co-Parenting Is Similar To Working With Co-Workers

Above we asked if your co-workers have been affected because of your divorce/separation. Co-workers and Co-parenting are very similar. How do you treat your co-workers? Are you nice, polite, and professional? Most likely you do not hug them, give them a kiss except on a special occasion. Most likely they treat you with respect. They too expect the same behavior in return. You would not cuss out a co-worker; tell them they are fat or ugly. You would definitely never touch, hit, push or threaten a co-worker, because you know that will land you in jail, fired, or dead. You would never sexually attack that person or talk dirty around them. Now look at the word Co-worker and Co-parent. Both are people that will be working with you. Notice the word "Co". When you think about your partner realize that your partner is now a working partner. You would never call your Co-worker names, slap them, degrade them; the same respect must be given to your spouse/partner. You need to start taking the emotional feelings out of your relationship and start seeing each other as Co-workers, Co-parents. This is the day; you might start looking at your spouse/partner differently. You can be friends, good friends, you can be partners. You cannot be lovers, destroyers, or mean to each other.

You would not act that way towards a Co-worker, and you cannot act that way towards a spouse/partner. Always treat your "ex" with respect, professionalism, and patience. Patience is important, because it might take time for them to learn what you have already figured out. They are the mother or the father of your child(ren). That in itself makes them very special people. There will never be a person who has given you or will give you such a wonderful gift. Reward that person for that fact alone. Honor them for the love they give your child(ren). Respect them because they gave you your family.

LOVE THEM BECAUSE YOU LOVE WHAT GREW FROM YOUR BODIES AND YOUR SOUL.

Notes:

Chapter 4 - A Healthy Divorce - How Do Children Learn

From birth to four years of age, your child(ren)'s caregivers were the main source and influence in their life. For the most part, the caregiver, usually the parents taught them responsibility, discipline, how to love, and how to receive love in return. They taught the child through different life experiences and day-to-day living. The parents are first and foremost role models in their child(ren)'s life. What we observed early in life; reflect in our lives today. The influence that our parents played in our life exhibits how we think and most importantly how we react with other people. From our surroundings, like a sponge, our brain squeezed in all that we could learn, as well as replicating; imitating learned behavior by watching our caregivers and mirroring their actions.

For example when you are driving, your child's first driving experience most likely occurred sitting in the back seat and watching you drive. Hopefully they were in a car seat. For fourteen years, from infant to teen, your driving skills were observed and perceived as correct driving behavior.

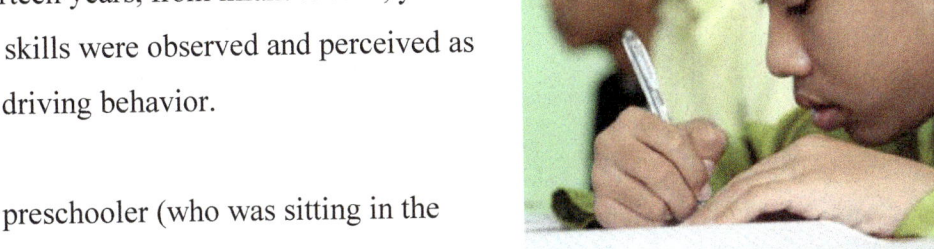

If your preschooler (who was sitting in the back seat) watched you speed, as you spoke on the phone telling the person on the other end you just got your car up to 90 miles an hour, most likely at 16 your child(ren) when driving, will see nothing wrong with speeding. In fact, because speeding was a learned behavior the once preschooler, now teenager most likely will not even realize they are in danger because of driving too fast. Sadly like their parent, they too are impressed by speed and how fast the car can go; they do not see that they are doing anything wrong. When a police officer pulls them over, they might in fact be a little put off, because they were doing nothing wrong. The police officer was just singling them out, giving them a hard time, perhaps because they were a teenager. On the other hand, if mom is a cautious driver and never showed anger when driving, the teen most likely will be a considerate driver. We learn from those we watch, people we observe. We are creatures on this earth that mimic the behaviors of others. That does not mean that if we as parents grew up in a dysfunctional family, our own family needs to follow the pattern set by our past life. Perhaps mom drank, and dad beat mom when she got intoxicated. That pattern and abuse must and can stop. We can change; we can break the cycle of abuse or inappropriate behavior. Negative learned behavior can be redirected. However, changing behavior takes time because you must retrain your brain while redirecting the behavior. Security word activities note word and page number. The family you will see in the video can change their behavior, and we all can become better people. Today is a perfect time to change something that we do not like about ourselves, especially if we have passed on a bad habit or trait.

Video "Dysfunctional Family"

WORKBOOK QUESTIONS,

(4-1) When do you believe this family started to play games with one another by using the child to communicate instead of communicating together as parents?

_____

_____

(4-2) Now that the child is in his teens, how can the parents re-establish their relationship, so they do not burden the child with their marital problems?

_____

_____

(4-3) This young teen will grow up some day and have relationships with other people. From watching his parents, what type of behavior and experiences will he take with him into adulthood?

(4-4) My changed life and habits I am going to change.
STARTING TODAY, PLEASE WRITE DOWN WHAT TRAITS OR BEHAVIORS CONCERNING YOURSELF YOU WOULD LIKE TO CHANGE, USE A CLEAN SHEET OF PAPER AND THEN HANG THE PAPER ON THE INSIDE OF YOUR CLOTHES CLOSET WHERE YOU CAN REFER TO WHAT YOU WROTE EVERY DAY. WE HAVE PROVIDED YOU A WORKSHEET IN YOUR WORKBOOK.

NOTES:

Thank you for your input.

Chapter 5 - A Healthy Divorce - Planning A Healthy Separation For The Children

Give them the gift of honesty.

Give them the gift of choice.

Give them the gift of patience and time.

Give them the gift of accurate information.

Give them the gift of trust.

Give them the gift of security and continuity.

Give them the gift of making them your highest priority!

1. GIVE THEM THE GIFT OF HONESTY.

Be honest with your child(ren) about the reasons for the decision to separate, but try to refrain from blaming, criticizing, or exaggerating. Let their ages guide you in what to say and how much to say. Be calm and sensitive to their difficult position. You are asking them to accept a decision that they will probably see as unacceptable, a decision they have no control over, no power to change, and no ability to refuse.

2. GIVE THEM THE GIFT OF CHOICE.

Allow them their own individual reactions. Don't try to make them less sad or less mad. Don't try to align them with your position on the separation. Don't try to give them your anger or hurt or need for revenge.

3. GIVE THEM THE GIFT OF PATIENCE AND TIME.

Answer all their questions openly, honestly, and as objectively as possible. Realize that they can register and process only pieces of your response at any given time and may feel compelled to ask the same questions over and over again so to process the thoughts from different angles. Children process information at different developmental levels. Try to be patient with this repetitive process.

4. GIVE THEM THE GIFT OF ACCURATE INFORMATION.

Try to give them information that will affect their eventual adjustment. Decide who will live where, in how big a place, in what school right at the start. Talk to them about how they will get to school, who will help them with their homework, how they can stay in touch with their friends. If they are late teens, and they plan to go on to higher education, decide how college or any other type of education will be handled. Also discuss other concerns, such as how to provide a car for their use. The more the child(ren) know, the less they will be depressed and anxious and the faster they will adjust.

5. GIVE THEM THE GIFT OF TRUST.

Don't' lie in order to save their feelings. Don't give hope where there is no realistic hope or fuel their fantasies of life being no different after a separation. A child(ren)'s sense of trust in their parents can be disrupted for a long time if lies or half-truths are told during this crisis.

6. GIVE THEM THE GIFT OF SECURITY AND CONTINUITY.

The process of selecting a second residence for one spouse to move into can be extremely important for child(ren)'s eventual adjustment. Children manage this difficult transition better when they are involved in the process of change. It may be useful to take child(ren) with you to look at new places. Get their input about size, location, neighborhood facilities, and so on. Try to be sensitive to their needs and feelings while keeping a realistic eye on financial considerations.

Although it's not always a good idea for the children to be present when the parent actually moves out, the timing of this move should not be a surprise. It is a good idea to have child(ren) help you move in and organize and decorate the new home. It is important to get their input about which toys, clothes, and furniture they would like to have at each home. If they are old enough, let them do some of their own packing.

Work with them to plan their new bedrooms and to create a cozy, warm atmosphere that will make them feel comfortable and wanted in their new place. Make sure all the children have some kind of space, bed, and drawers to call their own. If the space is small, create separate spaces with room dividers or creative placement of furniture. If money is a problem, shop for used furniture or unfinished furniture. Children will resist being in a home that feels cold, unfamiliar, and not kid-friendly.

7. GIVE THEM THE GIFT OF MAKING THEM YOUR HIGHEST PRIORITY.

Try your best to put the child(ren)'s needs above your own. Often what is best for the child(ren) is not what's best for the parent and vice versa. The child(ren)'s needs must be the higher priority. They are the helpless victims of your choices and these choices may influence their adjustment for years to come. Decisions in divorce areas are among the most important decisions you may ever make regarding your child(ren)'s well-being.

HOW TO PLAN A HEALTHY SEPARATION

Decide on the goals of the separation.

Decide on a reasonable time limit for the separation.

Decide which spouse is going to move out.

Negotiate financial responsibilities during the separation.

Decide on a residential access plan for the child(ren).

Decide how much time you want to spend with each other.

After everything is planned, tell the child(ren).

1. DECIDE ON THE GOALS OF THE SEPARATION.

Just as any task that you set your mind to, separation and divorce must be objectively structured with plenty of room for change and adjustment. It is best to set short term goals and long reaching goals. In the back of this program (Chapter 25), you will find a program on how to set goals. The reference worksheet works well to set up your goals. Plan out how you are going to accomplish your short and long term goals. Give yourself a starting date and an ending date. Work each day on your goals by using a Things-To-Do List, setting priorities and rewarding yourself when you accomplish not just your goals, but the singular items that need to be finished in order to complete your goals.

Things-To-Do List is not a punishment list. Its main function is to keep you on track as you finish your goals. It is a building block for task driven accomplishments. If you start your list and do not get everything done, don't get upset. Just move the items that you did not finish over to the next day or the next week. Try to work each day on your list at your pace. Celebrate when you cross off a task that was done well. Your list of accomplishments should always include doing something fun, down time, recreation with your kids as well as quiet and social time for yourself. Remember to prioritize your list. Paying bills must be an important part of your list. Put the items that are important at the top of your list with an asterisk.

Items that have stayed on your list for some time must become your priority. Always try to do the worst job first. People dread doing some jobs so much they start making excuses. So much so, they start stressing out about getting the job finished. Here is an example; cleaning the garage. Roberta had such a cluttered garage; in fact the family could not find their boat chairs. She made excuses how she hated to clean the garage because in the past she saw spiders crawling up the walls of the garage and she was scared of spiders. She said it would take all weekend to clean the garage and the kids had sporting events she had to attend. However, one rainy Saturday in spite of the spiders she got busy and cleaned the garage. Not making any excuses and putting her mind to it, the garage took two hours to clean even after seeing two spiders. Finding four boat chairs was well worth the hard work she put in. Think about how she consumed her time with dread and guilt as she spent procrastinating about a job she did not want to do. Instead, she should have done the worst job first and stopped putting the dreaded job of cleaning the garage off. For Roberta, the results would have been no stress or overwhelming feelings of dread.

Lastly, give credit where credit is due. If your child(ren) helped you complete your Things-To-Do List, give them credit and reward great behavior. Let them have a sense of achievement and allow them to experience the feeling of success and a job well done. There is nothing better to feel and experience triumph when you take on a task and complete a project. Let them rejoice in a joint effort when goals are achieved and jobs are done well.

2. DECIDE ON A REASONABLE TIME LIMIT FOR THE SEPARATION.

Separations should be defined for a specific time period, generally between one month and one year. Separations are not effective if they are open ended, meaning that they go on and on until one person gets tired of it. And they're not helpful if they only last a few days or weeks. Think about planning your separation in six to eight-week segments. How you may feel one or two weeks into a separation is not a reliable way to make a lasting decision. Separation evokes many new feelings and perceptions, and people need time to experience them. If you are seeing a counselor, the separating couple will review what the separation experience has been like for each of them usually at the end of eight weeks. Most likely three suggestions on how to proceed is suggested: continue the separation as is or with some modifications for another six to eight weeks; decide to discontinue the separation and make plans to reconcile with the eventual goal of moving back together again; redefine the separation with the intent of pursuing a divorce.

3. DECIDE WHICH SPOUSE/PARTNER IS GOING TO MOVE OUT.

Be realistic. Consider the needs and stability of the child(ren). It does not make much sense for a father who travels extensively in his work and is not available during daytime hours to insist on staying in the house. Nor is it appropriate for a mother who works only ten hours a week to move into a small apartment with three children. We have known some couples who have worked out an innovative plan where the child(ren) stay in the house and the parents alternate, one living in the house with the child(ren) for two weeks or a month at a time while the other lives in a nearby apartment, then the parents switch residences. This plan seems to work only with people who are able to get along well and are fairly flexible. Be careful when considering the size and location of the second residence. If the separation is likely to be a long one, more than two or three months, it's important that the second residence not feel like a motel or a cramped closet. The child(ren) will resist visiting this type of place and the parent who moved there is likely to feel a great deal of resentment. Of course it may be financially unrealistic to duplicate the home situation, but it's important to provide a comfortable feeling and sufficient room to accommodate everyone for an extended period of time.

This next segment is sometimes hard to emotionally think about. In divorce, the child(ren) are the most important consideration and their welfare/safety must first and foremost be taken into account. We have devised an access plan to help couples decide where the child(ren)'s primary residence should be. Even if you are sharing the child(ren) and working to develop a plan where the kids have access to both parents, certain logistics should be taken into account when developing your plan.
FIRST AND FOREMOST THE AGE OF THE CHILD(REN).

Judges in the past looked at a child(ren)'s age and if they were under five years of age, custody and primary residence overwhelmingly was given to the mother. Times have changed. Dads and moms work at home, work part time, or return home to live with parents. Mom's might find they need to go back to school so they can compete in the market place or mom now finds she has a reverse role and travels four days a week with her job.

Still, if a mom is breast feeding a two month old, both parents might look at that bonding time as so valuable to both mom and baby that dad might agree that mom may have the child(ren) during the week and then on weekends she agrees to use a breast pump or arranges a time to meet up with dad, so he can have the child(ren) and still enjoy bonding moments with his baby. Security word jurisdiction note word and page number.

Similar situation; where every weekend a soccer family travels to soccer games. Dad in the past drove his teenage son and his son's team mates to the games and helped coach the event for the past four years. Mom might find that if she wants to see her son on weekends and be a part of his life; she too must learn to coach and carpool young men to soccer practice and games on the weekends. Yes, she might at first be out of her comfort zone; however the volunteer job while challenging, could end up being fun.

WORKBOOK QUESTIONS,

(5-1) Take into consideration each child and their age. Who would be the best parent to have primary custody?

Mom's Pro's and Con's:

_____

_____

Dad's Pro's and Con's

_____

_____

Here are other important situations and circumstances that should be taken into account when forming a plan concerning where the child(ren) should live and what

days they should be with the other parent. Even if you are looking at shared equal custody, all of the following items should be taken into consideration when you are developing a parenting plan.

PLEASE LOOK AT EACH AREA OF INTEREST IF IT PERTAINS TO YOUR FAMILY, AND WRITE DOWN HOW YOU WOULD LIKE TO HANDLE EACH SITUATION.

(5-2) The closeness of the child(ren) and attachment to each parent:

_____
_____
_____

(5-3) How the child(ren) are handling the separation and divorce:

_____
_____
_____

(5-4) The residences of each parent: how far apart, size, and adequacy:

_____
_____
_____

(5-5) The location of school districts and the quality of education:

_____
_____
_____

(5-6) Difficulties in changing schools.

(5-7) The need for day care or baby-sitting:

(5-8) The need for after-school care or activities:

(5-9) Transportation from each residence to the schools:

(5-10) The work and travel schedule of the father:

(5-11) The work and travel schedule of the mother:

(5-12) The availability of backup babysitting for each parent:

(5-13) Other concerns you may have regarding parent access and where the child(ren) should live:

(5-14) Where will the child(ren) reside during the school week and on weekends? Be specific.

(5-15) Define specific days and times that they will live with the parent who is outside the household.

(5-16) How will transportation be shared?

Chapter 6 - A Healthy Divorce - Dealing With Clothes and Personal Articles

Your child(ren) are not guests in your home, they should not have to pack a bag. NEVER, EVER!! Children from a divorce family live in two homes, for example, one child may live on Maple Street and they also may live on River Road. They do not live in moms or dad's home; they live in their two homes. When a child(ren) stays in one or the other home, he should not pack a bag; bring his toothbrush, bike, or toys. Each home should have adequate clothes, books, education material, beds, closets, toys etc. The exception to that rule is if he/she just received a new toy or game and they want to show the other parent or play with the toy at the other home. Then that is perfectly all right for them to take it with them to their other home.

Apparel, for the most part, drives parents crazy. Let's say the child comes to his home on Maple Street wearing a new outfit that you just bought him. Sunday night comes and goes; the child comes back to River Road and guess what is not on his back, nor in a bag he carried his favorite toy home in. "THE NEW OUTFIT".

Now your "ex" has in their possession clothes that you bought for the child. Some would say, stop getting upset about the small stuff. Most would agree; except this type of behavior happens every single weekend.

WORKBOOK QUESTIONS,

(6-1) How would you handle this problem and what would you expect from your spouse/partner regarding leaving clothes, toys, and other property at the other house?

_____

_____

_____

_____

_____

_____

_____

_____

_____

_____

_____

Try to come up with a solution regarding left property going from one home to the other. Otherwise, this type of situation will continue to be frustrating.

Chapter 7 - A Healthy Divorce - Negotiate Financial Responsibilities During The Separation And Importance Of Play

Don't kid yourself: it is more costly operating two households, even if one is a small apartment.

Define who is going to pay which bills, and how.

Define who will pay for the child(ren)'s needs such as clothes and school activities during the separation period.

Budgeting for some is an art form. Thrifty consumers enjoy the challenge of getting the most out of every dollar. Sadly, as our economy shows many persons budget week to week, based on the money that was taken in the week before. When an emergency arises or someone misses just a few days of work, their budget is blown for weeks at a time. Accounting for money coming in and money going out is the most important task you must do when developing a budget. Below is a tool to help you see where your money is going. It is much harder to live and budget when one family is now living in two residences. Good luck, and don't forget to add to your budget that bag of popcorn you bought at the movie theatre for $10.99. Was it something you absolutely needed, or would it have been better to bring an apple and cheese snack from home?

Income Worksheet

Monthly Gross Income

Salary and wages	$_____
Bonuses and Fringe Benefits	$_____
Child Support	$_____
Alimony	$_____
Social Security	$_____
Retirement Income	$_____
Disability Payments	$_____
Unemployment	$_____
Worker's Comp	$_____
AFDC	$_____
Dividends	$_____
Interest Income	$_____
Business Income	$_____
Rental Income	$_____
Other income __	$_____

=$_____ **(copy this number to the right)**   Total Monthly Gross Income $_____

Deductions From Income

Taxes	$_____
Health Ins.	$_____
Other Deductions	$_____
Savings	$_____
401K	$_____

=$_____ **(copy this number to the right)**   Total Deductions From Income $_____

Monthly Available Income

Total Monthly Gross Income	$_____
(minus) Total Deductions From Income	-$_____

= $_____ **(copy this number to the right)**   Grand Total Monthly Available Income $_____

Expense Worksheet

When filling out this budget worksheet, if an expense is incurred less often than monthly, convert it to a monthly amount when calculating the monthly budget amount. For example, if an item occurs only once a year, divide the amount by twelve to get the monthly amount. Just be sure to allocate money from your income to cover that expense when it happens. A good example would be your tax bill on your property

Housing Expenses
Mortgage $_____
Home Insurance $_____
Property Taxes $_____
Repairs $_____
Rent $_____
Renters Insurance $_____
Lawn Care & Services $_____
=$_____ (copy this number to the right)   Total Housing Expenses $_____

Utilities
Gas $_____
Electric $_____
Phone $_____
Cable $_____
Water Trash $_____
Sewer $_____
Internet $_____
Cell Phone $_____
Storage Fees $_____
=$_____ (copy this number to the right)   Total Utilities $_____

Children
School Tuition $_____
School Lunches $_____
School Supplies Tutoring $_____
Team Fees $_____
School Photos $_____
Allowances $_____
Camps $_____
Recreation $_____
Sports Fees $_____
Babysitting $_____
Daycare $_____
Diapers $_____
Formula $_____
Child Support $_____
=$_____ (copy this number to the right)   Total Child Expense $_____

Financial

Bank Fees	$_____
Check Printing Fees	$_____
Safety Deposit Fees	$_____
Spending Cash	$_____
Bank Loan #1	$_____
Bank Loan #2	$_____
Student Loans	$_____
Auto Loans	$_____
Credit Card #1	$_____
Credit Card #2	$_____
Credit Card #3	$_____
Credit Card #4	$_____
Other	$_____

=$_____ (copy this number to the right)   Total Financial Expense $_____

Transportation

License Renewal	$_____
Gasoline	$_____
Auto Insurance	$_____
Tires	$_____
Maintenance/Oil Changes	$_____
Tolls	$_____
Taxi	$_____
Bus Fare	$_____

=$_____ (copy this number to the right)   Total Transportation Expense $_____

Health

Doctor	$_____
Dental	$_____
Eye Care	$_____
Annual Physical	$_____
Prescriptions	$_____
Glasses	$_____
Health Insurance	$_____
Life Insurance	$_____

=$_____ (copy this number to the right)   Total Health Expense $_____

Household /Pets

Groceries	$_____
Cleaning Goods	$_____
Office Supply	$_____

Pet Care $_____
Pet Boarding $_____
Vaccinations $_____
Supplies $_____
=$_____ (copy this number to the right) Total Household/Pet Expense $_____

Gifts
Holidays $_____
Birthdays $_____
Weddings $_____
Graduations $_____
General Cards $_____
Christmas Cards $_____
Wrapping Supplies $_____
Shipping $_____
=$_____ (copy this number to the right) Total Gift Expenses $_____

Personal
Eating Out $_____
Clothing $_____
Haircuts $_____
Nails $_____
Salon $_____
Magazines $_____
Newspaper $_____
Charities $_____
Club Dues $_____
Entertainment $_____
Movies $_____
Hobbies $_____
Dues/memberships $_____
Other $_____
=$_____ (copy this number to the right) Total Personal Expense $_____

Fee
Attorney Fees $_____
Accountant Fees $_____
Other Professional Fees $_____
=$_____ (copy this number to the right) Total Fee Expense $_____

Calculating Total Expenses on your budget worksheet

Total Monthly Expenses

Housing	$_____
Utilities	$_____
Children	$_____
Financial	$_____
Transportation	$_____
Health	$_____
Household	$_____
Gifts	$_____
Personal	$_____
Fees	$_____

=$_____ (copy this number to the right)   Grand Total Monthly Expense $_____

Is Your Budget Balanced?

To find out where you stand, subtract your total monthly expenses from your total monthly available income. If you come up with a negative number, you will need to work on cutting back on expenses.

Importance Of Play

Many times, we see only that the bills need paid, the grass needs cut, or the importance of going over 40 hours, because you need the overtime. Ask your child(ren) what is important to them? Do you think they are going to say, the car payment being paid, or spending time with you? Of course the car payment needs to be paid, homework needs to be completed and chores need to be finished. Saying that, play is important. Set aside time for relaxing, fun, and adventure when it comes to you and your child(ren) spending memorable time together.

Video "Importance of Play"

While planning your holidays and vacation; explore new exciting places that will be meaningful to your family; a vacation where memories are made and time is well spent. Include your child(ren) in the plans. Most of all, try to remember what it was like to be a kid during summer vacation. Close your eyes and remember back to a time, not so long ago when you were a kid, during summer break. For most, it was the best part of our childhood; going on vacation with our parents, hanging out at the park, or going swimming. Are your child(ren) experiencing all of the same wonderful times that summer has to offer? Regardless of your answer start today planning how you are going to spend your next vacation. It does not have to be expensive. Remember back to your own experience. What was best about your vacation with your parents? Vacations are all about family. Plan yours today!

Decide together how both you and your spouse/partner will spend holidays, vacations, weekends, and birthdays that occur during the time you have your child(ren). You might want to invest instead in two calendars, one for each spouse/partner. Both of you can enter at the same time your kid's schedule of events with your child(ren)'s goals both short term and long term for the entire year. Then both you and your spouse/partner will be able to set goals relevant to your children's particular activities, events, and interest.

Most likely there will be some dates or activities changed or cancelled throughout the year when scheduling times that far in advanced. However a calendar gives you a base to work from. Always be flexible and try to be accommodating. Thank you.

Your Summer Plans with the child(ren):

_____

_____

_____

_____

_____

Your Spouse's Summer Plans with the child(ren):

_____

_____

_____

_____

_____

Your Parent's (the Grandparent's) Summer Plans with the child(ren):

_____

_____

_____

_____

_____

_____

Your Spouse's Parent's (other Grandparent's) Summer Plans with the child(ren):

_____

_____

_____

_____

_____

_____

Special Summer Plans for the child(ren):

_____

_____

_____

_____

_____

_____

Chapter 8 - A Healthy Divorce - Decide How Much Time You And Your Spouse/Partner Want To Spend With Each Other

Couples need to communicate about their circumstance, parenting plan, and their child(ren). A couple of times a month schedule time to have lunch or dinner together. It is easier at first to spend time together out in public than in private. Continue if applicable your marital therapy sessions.

Establish boundaries so you can truly experience being separate. Unless you have advance permission, don't go to the other spouse's residence unannounced. Never go in when the other person is not there. Yes, that is or was your home, however currently it is not your residence, so always get permission to enter the property, even if your children are the only ones at home. Security word holiday note word and page number. If necessary, limit telephone calls to each other.

Don't spend nights together at the house. This will confuse the child(ren).

Decide in advance whether you are going to have sex with each other. Don't forget to bring a condom or contraceptive device to prevent pregnancy or the spread of a sexually transmitted disease. It sadly has happened to spouses/partners that somewhere (perhaps on a toilet seat; can you believe people have used that excuse) a spouse/partner contracted HIV or a sexually transmitted disease and gave it to their spouse/partner. It is important to have a discussion with your spouse regarding if you are sleeping around or whether it is acceptable to engage in sex with dates and if so, under what circumstances. With the current concern about sexually transmitted diseases, this is an important discussion to have!

Decide in advance whether either of you is free to date during the separation and under what circumstances. One couple that was continuing their separation after three months decided that it would be OK for each to kiss on a date; however intercourse would not be acceptable. Another couple decided that they would date but that they would not pick up partners in bars. Is it acceptable to tell the child(ren) you are dating other people, or for that matter should you have your date come to the home to meet your child(ren)? Try to experience really being separated. Stay out of each other's way. Don't follow each other around, don't third-degree each other about activities and whereabouts, and don't take your laundry home to be done even if you do it yourself.

AFTER EVERYTHING IS PLANNED, TELL THE CHILD(REN).

Chapter 9 - A Healthy Divorce - Child(ren) Need Honesty And Information During The Divorce Process

Don't demean or speak harshly of your spouse to or around the child(ren). Don't allow anyone else to do so.

Don't use the child(ren) as barter in your divorce negotiations. Don't say "You can have an extra day with the child(ren) if you increase your child support $100 per month" or "You can keep the house if I can have joint custody."

Develop an access system that allows for frequent and relatively equal time with the child(ren). Develop a predictable, consistent schedule that has the potential for occasional flexibility.

Encourage your child(ren) to express their feelings (negative and positive) freely, openly, and without any form of judgment or criticism from you.

Encourage a loving, supportive, quality relationship with the other parent.

Always make time to answer children's questions about divorce-related issues. Never lie but always consider the child(ren)'s ages and feelings in your response and in how much detail you give.

Don't pretend about your own feelings and don't try to give your feelings to your child(ren). It's all right to say, "I'm very angry with your father" but important to add "but that doesn't mean you need to be angry with him." Do not use your child(ren) to communicate with or spy on the other parent. Don't say, "Tell your father to stop calling me so much" or "Tell me all about Mom's new boyfriend." Don't interrogate your child(ren) about the details of the other parent's life or home. If they volunteer information, be pleasant and enthusiastic but don't ask for other details. If the child(ren) reports, "Guess what, Daddy has a new girlfriend." Don't say, "Oh really? What does she look like? How long has he known her? Does she stay overnight with him?" The correct response is, "Oh really? That's nice. Did you have fun this weekend?"

Be very careful how you handle your feelings about a new love interest of your former spouse. Security word transportation note word and page number. This person may someday be a stepparent for your child(ren) and what you say may cause him or her significant difficulties later on.

Don't refer to "that bitch" or "that jerk". Try to stay neutral if you can't be positive. Work with a therapist if your feelings are too severe. Don't burden your child(ren) so that in order to prove they love you they have to hate the new person in Mom's or Dad's life.

Chapter 10 - A Healthy Divorce - The Decision To Divorce

Up until this point, both partners were still examining the relationship and considering potential ways of repairing it. Even the distancing spouse hung on to some threads of hope. In the previous stages of separation couples dealt with the interplay of ambivalence and distancing leaving a slight hope for possible reconciliation. There was the experience of movement, interaction, loyalties, and even a sense of protection for each other and the family. Now this dance of pushing, pulling, hoping, and giving up comes to an end.

The most notable change that occurs here, and the most disruptive to achieving a healthy divorce, is the loss of an underlying sense of protectiveness between the spouses. Therapists call this a collusive bond.

WHAT IS A COLLUSIVE BOND AND HOW ALL COUPLES MUST MAINTAIN THIS BOND IF THEY WANT A HEALTHY DIVORCE?

All relationships that endure the first couple of years together develop this underlying and usually unspoken bond. It's a kind of "quid pro quo" if you protect my sensitive places, I will protect yours; I won't tell on you, if you don't tell on me. All spouses know intuitively the most sensitive and vulnerable parts of their partner. They know which buttons to push if they want to cause hurt. They also know how far to go and where to stop when arguments escalate. These are the boundaries of the collusive or protective bond. Even in the most conflicting relationships this bond usually remains intact.

Sometimes when one spouse is hurt badly by the other, such as by an affair, he or she will retaliate by threatening this bond. Still the decision to divorce is about the only event in a couple's life that can end this bond.

WHEN THE DECISION IS MADE, THE DANCE IS OVER. SPOUSES WILL SAY:

- "I never thought you would let it come to this."
- "I never believed you could do this to me and the child(ren)."
- "I feel betrayed and lonely."
- "You can't be the same person I loved."
- "You are my whole life, how could you do this?"
- "I don't even know who you are any more."

Of course, divorce does not have to destroy this bond. In fact, understanding how the bond is an essential ingredient of a healthy divorce establishes the trust while becoming co-parents. We have seen many couples that still feel supportive and protective of their former spouses five or ten years after their divorces, even though they have remarried and built new lives.

But when the decision to divorce is made, this bond is clearly threatened. The first assault often comes from the spouse who is left. The sense of rejection turns to anger and vengeance. Threats are made, money is taken from joint accounts, and the other spouse's relationship with the child(ren) and even extended family is sabotaged or threatened. Often attorneys are brought into the picture at this point, which adds another level to the threats and accusations. This also creates more pressure to break this bond as attorneys gear up to do battle and gather ammunition for the fight.

If you are the spouse who is leaving, you may have never expected the intensity of your partner's anger and retaliations. Try to remember that underneath all this emotion and hate are intense hurt and feelings of abandonment, rejection, loss and grief. This is why it is so important for divorcing couples to talk about all their feelings during the earlier stages.

WHEN YOUR SPOUSE/PARTNER TELLS YOU THEY WANT A DIVORCE; IT HURTS!!

This unexpected reaction by a spouse was demonstrated when Craig, a psychiatrist was asked to consult on a case with a fellow colleague. Here is the patient's story. "After years of conflict and unhappiness in their marriage, the wife had contacted an attorney and told the husband the marriage was over. The husband reacted by threatening to kill his wife and child(ren) and then himself, and had been immediately hospitalized. His wife proceeded with filing, and divorce papers were served on the husband in the hospital."

Holding the papers, the husband sobbed uncontrollably. "I never thought she would actually divorce me. She and the child(ren) were all I had. I worked hard all my life for them. She betrays me now that I'm close to retirement." He saw no reason to go on living.

The husband denied that he had meant any harm toward his wife or child(ren), but several guns were found at his home and no one will ever know if he would have hurt his family in a moment of rage. Fortunately, during the hospitalization he was able to look past the marriage and identify some new directions for himself. Regretfully his behavior and threats towards his family damaged his relationship with his children, so much so that it took nearly a year to repair the hurt and harm he caused his child(ren) and spouse.

CUSTODY FIGHTS OVER THE CHILD(REN)

The breakdown of this protective bond can also be seen clearly when divorcing parents get into custody fights over the child(ren). Often the ugliest side of the divorce process emerges here. The legal system, which we will discuss in the next chapter, unwittingly provides the arena that pits parent against parent. To the victor go the child(ren) but often with irreparable damage to all.

DO YOU KNOW PARENTS THAT MADE UP CHARGES THAT WERE FALSE, TO GET CUSTODY OF THEIR CHILD(REN)?

The implicit rules of surviving a fight over the custody of your child(ren) dictate that the former protective bond between you and your partner must be set aside. You are on your own. You may want to make your spouse look as bad and as dangerous as possible while at the same time protecting your own image as a parent. It is an unpleasant and destructive process that damages both parents and child(ren).

Old issues that were never mentioned during the marriage may now be made public by your partner. Some people even make charges that they know are either exaggerated or totally false. Suddenly you may find the same kind of accusations coming out of your mouth:

HERE ARE SOME ACCUSATIONS THAT THE COURTS HAVE HEARD OVER THE YEARS THAT WERE EXAGGERATIONS AT BEST, AND SOME PARENT'S GOING SO FAR AS TO COMMIT PERJURY WHEN THEY LIED TO THE COURT.

- Suspected affairs, now or years ago, having an abortion in the past,
- Abusive behavior toward the child(ren), such as hitting your son with a belt or pulling your daughter's hair,
- Charges of incest,
- Impotency,
- Suspected homosexuality, frigidity,
- Sexual perversions such as cross-dressing or wearing opposite-sex underwear,
- Stealing at work,

- Alcoholic or abusive parents,
- Alleged sexual molestation of your child(ren).

The last item on our list above represents the epitome of the breakdown of the protective bond between couples. This allegation of molestation has become so common in custody disputes over the past decade that a whole collection of books and articles have been written to help professionals understand and deal with it. This is perhaps the ultimate charge, and it will debase and cloud the image of a parent for the rest of his or her life.

Some questions and answers that might help you when communicating with your child(ren), family, or friends. Please answer these questions on a separate piece of paper. Do not go to your workbook. These questions are meant to start the thinking process that "I am not married any more, this is a business relationship from here on out, and I need to regard our past marriage now as a business relationship trying to leave the emotional part of the relationship behind and begin thinking about what is best for my children."

QUESTION: 10 (A)
How do we maintain the Collusive Bond if my spouse left me, and is not paying child support? I have been left to raise the child(ren) on my own. I have a right to tell my family what a lousy spouse she is. If it was not for the so-called-friend (that she spent

thousands of dollars on) she had an affair with for the last three years of our marriage, my child(ren) would have had enough money to go to college.

HOW WOULD YOU ANSWER THIS QUESTION

ONE WAY TO HANDLE THE SITUATION, ANSWER FOR QUESTION 10 (A)

You take care of it through the courts. It is not your kids business, the neighbors business, or your family's business that your wife had a three year affair and spent all the money on a boyfriend. To retain the Collusive Bond you must maintain your silence. This is hard to do. Your spouse hurt you and hurt your child(ren). If you need someone to talk to perhaps speak with a minister or best friend that can maintain your confidence.

Stick to the issues. The spouse has not been paying child support. It is your child(ren)'s money; to maintain a lifestyle they deserve. Based on a court order that you received; your spouse has an obligation to pay support. You can go after the support payments, but leave what could destroy your spouse's reputation and the relationship she has with your kids alone.

QUESTION 10 (B):

My child(ren) are upset because their father does not come to see them. Should I tell them he is in jail for not making child support payments?

HOW WOULD YOU ANSWER THIS QUESTION?

ONE WAY TO HANDLE THE SITUATION, ANSWER FOR QUESTION 10 (B)

No they really do not want to know their father would rather go to jail, than pay child support.

I understand your concern. For the most part, you now have a duel role as mother and father. You will have to be the provider that loves, disciplines, and supports your child(ren)'s every need. Big responsibility. Until dad is released and hopefully realizes his responsibilities encourage your child(ren) to remember the good times that they had with their father. If they were too young to remember, tell them stories about your pregnancy. How they were born, and how much you loved them when they came into this world. Talk about their childhood and the cute things they did. Most of all, tell them you love them, and that mommy is going to be both mommy and daddy until they see daddy again. Lastly; often after kids do not see their parents for a long period of time, they forget what their parent looks like. Child(ren) will feel sad and confused that they do not remember their parents face or the color of their hair. Bring out an old album with pictures of dad and allow your child to put a picture of their father in their room to show their friends that they too have a father, and to remind your son what their father looks like.

QUESTION 10 (C)

I am furious with my husband and I want my friends and family to know what he has done to us. I am angry because my husband has not seen my son in over a year. What are my options; do you think I should tell my parents and friends about what I have to put up with?

HOW WOULD YOU ANSWER THIS QUESTION?

ONE WAY TO HANDLE THE SITUATION, ANSWER FOR QUESTION 10 (C)

It would make sense that you feel a lot of anger toward your child(ren)'s father because your son is hurting. Most likely it probably won't help you to dwell on those feelings for long and it won't help your son to share your angry feelings with him. The tricky part here is that your son needs to have a 'good story' in his head about his father. All kids need this. You can help with this by telling your son how he and his Dad are alike and what you knew of and liked about his father when you met him. It will not help your son, even in this situation to only think bad things about his father. Plus it won't make sense to him that you were attracted to someone 'bad'. Your son, might analyze that if mom thinks my dad is a bad person, I must be a bad person too, because I am my father's son.

You certainly can also say to your son that you're sorry this has happened to him and try to comfort him when he is confused, angry, or grieving. As far as an explanation, you really don't have one and you're probably better off expressing puzzlement to your son about your husband's behavior. You don't understand why his Dad is not seeing him right now. Being puzzled sends the message that it does not makes sense that someone would not want to know him. Yes, it is better to act puzzled, than to give him a story that he is sick or traveling out of the country. Never lose hope, but living on hope may be destructive.

What we suggest is this, sit down with your child(ren) and at the same time "Scratch your head." Yes you are skeptical about how your spouse/partner is acting, yet this is an idea and an approach you might think about taking. "Scratch your head" and say to your child(ren) "I do not understand why he/she is not here for you right now, it does not make sense, he loves you very much." Keep scratching, "I just do not understand it", use the word perplexed if your child(ren) are a little bit older. For a younger child assist him in putting his hand on his head and tell him to "Scratch his head." Every time he/she thinks of the other parent and is sad or confused, he/she needs to put their hand on their head where we think, not to our heart, where we feel and "Scratch our head". We think with our brains, as we say to our self "I don't understand his/her behavior", (meaning dad's or mom's behavior). "I am a great kid, he/she loves me so much, so I am scratching my head because I am total puzzled because of his/her behavior."

QUESTION 10 (D)

I want to tell the judge how my wife was a terrible person during the time we were married. In fact towards the end of our marriage, she went to bars after work and left me to take care of the child(ren).

A Healthy Divorce

HOW WOULD YOU ANSWER THIS QUESTION?

ONE WAY TO HANDLE THE SITUATION, ANSWER FOR QUESTION 10 (D)

Some states look at grounds for divorce as moral issues. Can morals be legally judged? What is moral to one person is not moral to another. However different courts look at different situations. We always suggest you seek advice prior to filing for a divorce. An attorney should be able to give you information to better inform you about your legal rights and if you have legal grounds to go to court.

Private mediation also is good for the family that wants to have a neutral person help them to decide what is best for their family. If your state allows mediation call a mediator and sit down with that person, to work out your parenting agreement. Once finished, you can submit the agreement to the court yourself or go to an attorney and the attorney will file the agreement both parties have agreed upon.

QUESTION 10 (E)

While taking this class a man learns about the Collusive Bond and later confesses in a letter to the school that he was so mad at his wife that he just wanted to get back at her. He commented, "I told everyone, our friends, my family, people she worked with, secrets that my wife told me about her family and now she will not talk to me. What should I do?"

HOW WOULD YOU ANSWER THIS QUESTION?

ONE WAY TO HANDLE THE SITUATION, ANSWER FOR QUESTION 10 E

I can feel just from your letter how much pain you are in. Yes, you did break the Collusive Bond. No doubt about it. It all comes down to trust. The bond is an agreement; it is an agreement to trust. This time the trust has been broken. The way you fix trust is to figure out why it was so important to tell her secrets to everyone who would listen. Once you have established why you did it, confront her, tell her why you did it, and ask for forgiveness. Humans when hurt, lash out. You were hurt and you lashed out, not thinking about the consequences. Saying you're sorry is only part of the repair. You must show her you are sorry and do everything in your power to make it right. Ask for her trust one more time. Time does cure a lot of heartache. Monthly, go to her and ask for forgiveness, ask for her trust. When and if you get it back appreciate the gift that she has given you. Never betray her again. Start trying to communicate your feelings or seek professional help regarding what you are going through.

PLEASE READ BELOW THE INFORMATION ON COLLUSIVE BONDS AND READ THE AGREEMENT THAT IS ATTACHED TO IT.

You may copy the agreement and what you wrote for your own use. This agreement will not be recorded on your computer. If you ever want to destroy the agreement, you may do so. It is for your use only. If you want to share it with your spouse/partner, you may do so. Remember, you are going through a divorce. Anything you say or write can be used in court against you. If you feel you cannot share this part of the program with your spouse/partner, please use good judgment regarding what you say when you have contact with him/her.

Next, is an agreement that you might want to look at, add to and sign. You do not have to do this exercise. If you decide to do it, you do not have to give it to your spouse/partner. You can keep it, to remember a promise you want to keep. You can give it to your spouse/partner to educate them about the Collusive Bond. Most people do not understand the strong meaning behind it and how breaking the bond can affect couples for years or a lifetime to come.

If you have broken the bond, you might want to talk to your spouse/partner about why you broke their trust and apologize if that is the appropriate response concerning your mistake or lack of judgment. However, if you have not broken the message behind the Collusive Bond, celebrate and go one step further; promise yourself that no matter what, or how bad it gets, you will not betray the Collusive Bond.

Thank you and work hard thinking about what you want to add to your Lifetime Loyalty Agreement. Put the agreement somewhere where you can refer to it often. When you are stressed or mad at your spouse/partner, bring out the agreement to remind yourself that above all you have done the right honorable thing.

ACADEMY FOR A HEALTHY DIVORCE

THIS IS A LIFETIME LOYALTY AGREEMENT BETWEEN YOU AND YOUR SPOUSE. CAN AN AGREEMENT BE REACHED BETWEEN YOU AND YOUR SPOUSE TO MAINTAIN THIS FAMILY LOYALTY AND TRUST AGREEMENT? I, _____ AGREE TO PROTECT MY FAMILY TRUST AND WILL CONTINUE TO VALUE THE FAMILY COLLUSIVE BOND THAT WAS ESTABLISH YEARS AGO BETWEEN MY SPOUSE/PARTNER AND MYSELF. FURTHER MORE, I HOPE THAT ONCE THIS DIVORCE IS FINALIZED:

_____
_____
_____
_____
_____
_____
_____

NAME_____ DATE_____

Chapter 11 - A Healthy Divorce - Developing A Parenting Plan

Things that will be discussed in this chapter are:

- How to mediate.
- Types of custody arrangements.
- Access during summers, holiday, and school year.
- A few questions and suggestions regarding access during school year.
- When those fun days of summer are over and the kids are enthusiastically anticipating the first day of school, some points should be covered to keep both parents informed.
- Living in close proximity to your child(ren)'s school.

HOW TO MEDIATE

SIX WAYS TO LOSE A DISAGREEMENT

Why can't we all just get along? Oh, that's right – because we're human. Being individuals with our own unique attitudes, ideas, and opinions is generally a good thing. However, it can also be the breeding ground for conflict in relationships, whether that relationship is with your partner or ex. This advice is excellent when working with your children. One of the best ways to teach your children how to disagree is to teach them how to argue fair.

With disagreements sometimes come arguments.

The two are never far from each other. So what should you do, or more importantly not do, when those unavoidable disagreements turn into quarrels?

Here are six surefire ways to make sure you lose the argument:

1. Yell At The Other Person. When we lose control of our volume, we've also lost control of our emotions. Let the argument become a screaming match, and you'll completely lose focus on the issue at hand as you each attempt to out-yell each other. Keeping your voice at a moderate level volume, or even dropping it down a bit, can have a calming effect on a potentially escalating situation.

2. Change The Subject. Now is not the time to bring up every other beef you've ever had with this person. Stay focused on the issue at hand. If there are other legitimate issues that need to be resolved, save them for another time. For now, it's important to be single-minded and work towards resolving the one dispute that triggered the argument.

3. Refuse to Accept Responsibility. Don't blame the other person. It's important to recognize your own potential contribution to the problem. Reflect on how your own actions may have added fuel to the conflict. Be willing to accept responsibility, and ask for forgiveness for your role in the issue. Playing the blame game doesn't get us any closer to resolving conflict. Ask the question, and also answer it yourself; yes right there in the middle of the argument. Say something like, "let's have a time out and ask ourselves, if we could do it all over again, how would you have handled the situation, problem?" Then add, once you give me your answer, I would like to give you my answer.

4. Bring Up Past Mistakes. Avoid reminding the other person of every past offense they've ever committed. Let them recover from their errors and feel assured that any forgiveness you've given in the past was completely genuine. Holding on to hurt and letting it become a grudge only hurts you in the end.

5. Launch Personal Attacks. When you focus on the other person's character rather than the issue you're disagreeing about, you're disrespecting them, not disagreeing with them. Don't attack who you think they are (lazy, incompetent, forgetful, selfish, etc.); instead, focus on their behavior. This keeps the argument on topic and prevents it from becoming personal.

6. Correct Their Grammar. When all else fails, it's tempting to resort to something really petty. Avoid the temptation to point out their dangling participles or double

negatives. When we resort to attacking trivial issues, it indicates we've totally lost our focus and self-control, and even worse it rings of desperation.

Disagreements in life are inevitable, but they don't always have to lead to an argument or conflict. However, when they do, avoiding these six surefire ways to lose an argument can lead to greater success in your conflict resolution attempts. In the end, our goal shouldn't be to win the argument but rather to find a mutually agreeable resolution for all parties involved. Here's to more successful conflict (disagreement) resolution for us all.

HOW TO WIN A DISAGREEMENT

We all have that friend, family member, spouse, or perhaps look in the mirror; who loves to argue. You know exactly who I'm talking about; the one who frustratingly has a comeback for everything you say, regardless of how absurd it is. They always seem to get under your skin; just THINKING about them gets you fired up.

You would LOVE to best them in an argument, just once. You feel like that satisfaction would put you on top of the world but HOW can you achieve it?

To start looking at this problem, we must break it down. People argue to try and get their point across to YOU, to try to change YOUR mind on something, or to try and put themselves above YOU. They have no ammunition if you remove YOURSELF from the equation, and turn the focus towards THEM. Now how do you accomplish this, you might ask, without just getting up and walking away from the argument?

In order to begin disarming your opponent, actually listen to what they say. Do NOT think about what you are going to say next, listen to what they are saying, and ask them clarifying questions. Do not assume you know exactly what they are talking about, because there is a chance that you are arguing about nothing, due to a simple lack of understanding of each other. Do not underestimate the Law of Reciprocation, if you make an effort to understand them, they will likely reciprocate and try to understand you. You and your nemesis will tranquilize each other with clarifications and understanding.

To further remove their combative behavior, you must remove your ego. Nothing disarms an opponent more than your indifference towards who is the "winner" of the argument. At some point of the argument you must decide: am I arguing to feel good about myself, or to get a point across? Do you really think that beating an arguer in one argument is going to give you lasting personal validation? Sure, for maybe about five minutes. Feeling that you need the validation of another person, in the form of beating them in an argument, is a very low-status behavior. If you're a smooth, charming fellow, and you lose an argument, you're still going to still be a smooth, charming fellow. They're still going to be an argumentative piece-of-work.

If you still absolutely MUST convince your opponent of something, don't try to corner them or make them feel threatened. Throughout the animal kingdom, animals such as sharks, bears, and bees will not attack you unless they feel threatened. The more you threaten your opponent, the more defensive they will get, and it will be harder to get your point of view across. They will put up thick walls defending themselves, and will care less about what you have to say. One of the best ways to prevent coming across as threatening is to keep a calm demeanor throughout the argument. Keep an even, slow, and low voice tonality; along with non-threatening body language; do not stare down, point, or cross your arms. As tension escalates, it will become increasingly difficult to think rationally. Losing your temper is very childish and will likely accomplish nothing. Aim for solid eye contact while delivering a slow, powerful message.

It is important to note that not all arguments are negative. I'm not saying you should never argue. Sometimes it can be fun to argue and you can certainly learn a lot from others. You will find that none of these strategies will work if you are simply trying to win an argument for the sake of winning. If that is your goal, then sorry, I can't help you. If you find yourself arguing with one of these people, it will be next to impossible to crumble them. It's not worth wasting your breath if you are trying to get something done, and they are just trying to win. Consider these strategies next time you find yourself in an argument, and you will find yourself a winner.

THE POSITIVES TO MEDIATION

If you have a computer, please watch the below link on how to mediate.

http://www.wikihow.com/Mediate-Family-Arguments

One of the biggest challenges we all face is dealing effectively with the differences we have with other people. These differences can range from small scale disagreements, which can build up over time and put a strain on any relationship; to larger conflicts which could potentially wind up in a court of law. In addition, differences can arise with anyone in our life, from our spouse or significant other, to our friends and neighbors, to our co-workers and business partners, and so on.

Although conflict is a natural part of life, fighting can imperil our happiness at home, our effectiveness at work, and our overall sense of well-being.

By acquiring skills to de-escalate conflict and to resolve disputes amicably, you'll be taking a proactive approach to building a better life for yourself and for those around you.

Mediators are third parties who help people solve their disagreements. They help parties who are involved in a conflict to communicate more effectively and to explore possible ways of moving forward. By learning the basic skills used by mediators to help others get to the core of disputes and resolve them, you can begin to mediate your own disputes. Below you'll find an introduction to some of the most basic skills you need to learn to introduce mediation as a conflict resolution method in your life.

SIT DOWN TO TALK ABOUT THE PROBLEM WITH A WILLINGNESS TO RESOLVE IT.

To resolve a disagreement, each party should be willing to contribute to the conversation. Instead of taking a firm stance while focusing on your position, each side during the exchange of dialogue should express their interest, needs, and concerns. Sometimes it helps each other to focus on what your specific desires, fears, and aspirations are that underlie each side's position.

ESTABLISH GROUND RULES

A lot of the time the problem is not so much in the nature of any individual dispute but in the way in which differences are handled. Mediation helps people change the way in which they interact with others and the way in which they respond to conflict. When you sit down with someone in an attempt to resolve a disagreement, you should start out by establishing ground rules to create a space of tolerance and respect in which you can iron out your differences. Ground rules can include things such as the following:

Each side will take turns speaking. In addition, each person gets a predetermined period of time to speak, during which they cannot be interrupted by the other. If the other hears something that they want to respond to and it's not their turn to speak, they should write it down and wait until it's their turn to say it.

Only one person can get angry at a time. Write down how you will achieve this skill.

Focus on one issue at a time. Write down what you want to talk about and put each issue in an order of preference.

[blank lined writing area]

Establish a statute of limitations on old grievances. That is, don't bring up events that occurred two years ago.

Refrain from using phrases such as "You always . .", or "You never . ."

Try not to blame the other person, speak for the other person, or speculate about the motives of the other.

Refrain from name-calling.

Treat each other with respect.

TAKE RESPONSIBILITY FOR YOUR ACTIONS.

Each side should strive to take responsibility for their contribution to the conflict. Ask the person who you are mediating with, how would you have done this different? You too must answer the same questions.

How would I have done this different, if I had a chance to do it over again?

[blank lined writing area]

Ask the other person, how would you have done this different, if you had a chance to do it over again?

SEPARATE THE PEOPLE FROM THE PROBLEM

The process of mediation rests on the expectation that every person has an element of goodwill and integrity, and that everyone is capable of change. When trying to resolve a dispute, it's very important that you don't identify the other person as being the problem, for example: "The problem is that he's selfish", "The problem is that she's a spendthrift", and so on. When you identify the other person as being the problem, this creates a "me versus you" atmosphere, in which animosity is likely to arise. By separating the people from the problem both parties can focus on jointly attacking the problem, instead of attacking each other.

DEVELOP THE SKILL OF ACTIVE LISTENING

A human being needs to feel understood and active listening will help you to understand the message the other person is trying to convey. When it's the other person's turn to speak make sure that you listen to them attentively.

Remain focused on what the other is saying instead of rehearsing in your head what you're going to say next. Use paraphrasing to make sure that you understand what the other has just said; paraphrasing basically means that when the other person is finished talking you repeat in your own words what you heard them say. You can use a phrase like the following: "Let me see if I understand what you're saying: I'm going to repeat what I just heard you say in my own words, and please feel free to correct me if I misinterpret anything you've said."

Encourage the other person to elaborate on what they're saying and to get everything they're feeling off their chest; ask for clarifying information. Security word communication note word and page number. Remember that understanding is not synonymous with agreeing.

PRACTICE EMPATHY

Try to see the world from the perspective of the other person, that is, put yourself in the shoes of the other. Be curious about the other person and about the thinking process that they followed to reach their conclusions. We all see the world differently based on our background, our experiences, our values, and our belief system. Seek to understand how the other sees the world, their motivations, and their aspirations.

LEARN TO EXPRESS YOURSELF

In resolving any disagreement with another it's important not only that you listen to the other and try to understand where they're coming from, but that you also express how you feel and let the other know what you really want. Communicate to the other side what you're experiencing, what your desires are, what's important to you, and tell them what your interests are.

CONCLUSION

Once you've identified each side's interests you can come up with creative ways to satisfy them. Stop looking for a single best answer, come up with as many solutions as possible, and don't assume that there's a fixed pie. The goal is for each party to walk away from a "mediation session" feeling understood and that an effective plan has been agreed upon for resolving the dispute and moving forward. Both need to have a clear understanding of exactly what the agreement entails, and both parties need to make a firm commitment to uphold their end of the bargain.

Think of ways to make sure that this problem, and others like it, won't arise again in the future.

By now, we hope, you have started thinking about mediation; let's put your skills to work.

THRU MEDIATION, TODAY WE ARE GOING TO MEDIATE ITEMS THAT WE CAN NOT RESOLVE.

You can apply mediation skills not only to help yourself resolve the conflicts in your own life, but also to help others resolve their disputes. Once you feel comfortable using mediation skills you can help mediate problems between you and your spouse, partner, or maybe even your children.

Wouldn't it be great to create a reputation for yourself as a peacemaker?

Part of this program is designed to give you an opportunity to think about how you want to set up your custody agreement and parenting plan. If your spouse/partner is taking the same class with you, it would be an excellent time to sit down together to discuss how you wish to address custody and parenting issues. Your court divorce packet will cover questions we will be talking about today. All of the courts questions must be addressed and for most items, some sort of resolution from both of you will have to be agreed upon.

This chapter is an excellent way to begin focusing on very important decisions. If you have a computer, please watch the below link on how to mediate.
http://www.wikihow.com/Mediate-Family-Arguments The link will show ways for you and your spouse/partner to mediate together, your own divorce and separation agreement. Key phases for mediation:

Follow the prescribed steps:

- Name the issue
- Other person(s) respond to the issue, for or against.

- Each hears the other's opinion and/or ideas.
- Both reflect on the other's opinion by stating, "This is what I hear you are saying."
- Each person takes their turn and brain storms, giving different ideas to resolve the issues or problems. Some refer to this phase as sharing ideas and opinions. This is not a time for arguments or accusations.
- Both or all persons review all of the options and choose the option that is best for all parties. Sometimes, taking each person's idea, (in part) works when all share one-another's ideas, as you come up with one decision.
- Both need to negotiate options or decide to go with a trial period for separate idea options.
- Take action. Reevaluate the option over time. If you decided to try a trial option, decide whose trial option you are going to do first.
- Try the second option to see if that idea could work as well.
- Reevaluate both decisions and come to a conclusion.
- Establish options, ideas, or decisions into your parenting plan and/or contract.

TYPES OF CUSTODY ARRANGEMENTS

Here are the definitions on what each and every description means when it comes to Custody Agreements:

Joint custody is now recognized in most states and in many jurisdictions is favored or mandated by the court. So if you live in one of those states and you don't want joint custody, one or both parents must object and convince the court that it won't work.

Joint custody is simply the definition that both parents will continue in the eyes of the law as equal partners in the process of raising the child(ren), just as when they were married. Joint custody does not define how much time the child(ren) spend with each parent. It can become more complicated than this. In most states there are independent definitions of joint legal and joint physical custody.

Joint legal custody means that both parents will have the right to share in the major decisions that will affect their child(ren)'s lives. This involves education, health and medical issues, religious preferences, and their social environment. Of course these decisions must be made jointly. When parents cannot agree or negotiate such choices, there are usually provisions in the final divorce agreement that spell out how such disagreements will be handled. For example, a mediator or counselor could negotiate disputes in this area, or one parent could be specified as making the final decision.

Joint physical custody has several variations. Primary physical custody designates whom the child(ren) will live with the majority of the time and which parent will make the everyday decisions for the child(ren) on such things as haircuts, dental appointments, and dance lessons. In some states this is more accurately termed primary physical residence. It may seem something of a contradiction to award parents joint legal custody and then turn around and define one parent as physical custodian. This policy stems from the courts' and legislatures' concern for protecting the stability of the family and household environment, particularly for young child(ren). Some states will enforce the definition of physical custody more than others.

Things can get even more complicated because the physical custody may also be defined as shared, split, or alternating.

Shared physical custody means parents have the child(ren) with them approximately half the time. In this designation, neither parent is presumed to have any sole decision making power. Day-to-Day decisions are made by whoever is the residential parent when the situation arises.
This type of custody requires a great deal of communication and cooperation between parents, who must be fairly adept at solving conflict and resolving disputes. It also helps if they have similar styles of parenting and similar values about raising their child(ren).

Split physical custody means that both parents are awarded physical custody at separate but specific times of the year. An example would be physical custody with the father from January through June and with the mother from July through December. A more common pattern is physical custody with one parent during the school year and the other parent during the summers. Thus, if the child(ren) live with the father during the school year in Virginia, physical custody would be with him for that period and then with the mother in California during the summers.

Alternating physical custody is very similar and in some states would not be seen as different from split physical custody. It means that physical custody would be defined as alternating between the parents in some predetermined and consistent way. In states where physical custody must be designated separately from joint custody, it could simply mean that the parent with whom the child(ren) are in residence is defined as having physical custody.

While these two categories may be confusing, they are usually employed for technical reasons in a legal context to achieve or define equal or balanced power in a divorce settlement. Try not to be confused here; in most cases these designations do not really define the access plan or where the child(ren) are living at a given time.

Sole custody was the traditional model of custody for many decades, based on an early, somewhat uniformed belief that child(ren) need the security and stability of staying in one place. It means that only one parent is awarded the legal and physical custody of the child(ren). This parent has complete control of all decisions about child(ren) rearing. The non-custodial parent has no legal rights with the child(ren) except the designated time to visit. In many states the non-custodial parent will not be allowed to see school or medical records for their child(ren) and cannot even sign for the child(ren)'s medical treatment without a written consent document from the custodial parent.

You need to know that many traditionally trained judges, attorneys, and therapists still favor this model. For the most part, we are seeing parents preferring shared custody where parents are equal taking part raising their child(ren).

ACCESS DURING SUMMERS, HOLIDAY, AND SCHOOL YEAR

In the earlier chapter we talked about how important play is for you and your child(ren). Create and plan activities that you can do with your child(ren) and design those activities around your access plan with them. You can use the following ideas for vacations and holidays or come up with your own ideas that better suit your family's life style.

For most kids, rich or poor, adventurous or computer savvy, they all love summer! They enjoy planning activities and doing fun and rewarding games, including sports. Remember back to a time where you could not wait until school was out and summer got underway. Or the thrill of leaving school on Friday, because there were going to be lots of fun things to do throughout the weekend. Each of us experienced different lives, yet if we would think back to our own days of summer or weekends, most likely we would remember some of these great activities that happened in our own life:

- swimming,
- going to the library,
- camp,
- riding bikes,
- summer school,
- sports,

- being with parents, and going on vacation,
- kite flying,
- play days with their friends,
- summer nights and catching lightning bugs,
- slumber parties,
- picnics,
- movies,
- parks,
- pools,
- going to the lake,
- fishing or skipping stones,
- church camp and bible school,
- religious and cultural activities
- learning to drive,
- internship,
- visiting colleges,
- being an exchange student or inviting one into your home,
- learning a new musical instrument or new hobby, just to name a few.

Your child(ren) hopefully will be able to enjoy some of the activities described above. Just as you shared encounters with your parents in your childhood, during your summer vacation/weekends; as co-parents, you will want to continue to share the same experiences in your kids' life as well. Sharing means; spending time with your child(ren); getting involved in meaningful activities during their childhood.

For some child(ren) an extended stay vacation with the other parent might be one of the highlights of the vacation. Plans do not just happen. It is important to make your family plans concerning where the kids are going to stay and what they are going to do and hope to accomplish at least six months to a year in advance. Some camps and other programs book up early, so early planning will give your child(ren) the opportunity to enroll in activities that they are interested in. Airplane fares are cheaper as well when you plan early.

Similarly, weekend visitation, teacher's planning days where kids are out of school, birthday and special days associated with your family festivities, holiday breaks, such as Christmas vacation, Easter, Thanksgiving, summer break as well as other religious and cultural holidays should be planned well in advanced, so there will be no misunderstandings or disappointed hurt feelings. Child(ren) should look forward to the planned activates that you have developed. Make sure you give the kids an opportunity to help plan the events. If planning these events are too difficult or you are not communicating with your spouse/partner as well as you would like, call in a mediator; as a neutral. They will help both of you come to a decision on how you want to negotiate your events/activates.

Be creative in planning activities where both parents will feel that they are getting their fair share in contributing to their child(ren)'s development. For example: if it is your week to have the child(ren), you might be considerate to your spouse when you find out that one of the days you have your child(ren) is your spouse's/partners birthday. Eagerly, share that day with her, by allowing the child(ren) to be with their mother; and don't forget to wish her a happy birthday. At certain times of the year, you and your spouse/partner might want to have the child(ren) on the exact same day. A negotiated solution might be that you will have the child(ren) from 9 to 3 in the afternoon and your spouse will pick the child(ren) up at 3 and keep the child(ren) for the remainder of the day. The next year you might agree to switch times. Try to have an open mind through compromise and commitment where both you and your spouse are dedicated to the up-bringing of your child(ren).

In today's world communication between families is vital to pull off a busy and packed schedule that most parents and child(ren) subscribe to day in and day out. An example: you and your mother are planning a wedding in May where your mom's next door neighbor (your childhood friend) is getting married. In fact your child(ren) graciously volunteered to help out serving the food after the ceremony. Your parents live out of state and having the kids and your parents together at such a happy occasion was something you have looked forward to for months. Out of the blue one of your child(ren) excitedly announces they have been invited to the prom. Not surprisingly this circumstance could cause a family dilemma, where one parent and perhaps the child could develop hurt feelings. Had the parents looked ahead, recognized that someone most likely would be asking their daughter to the prom, the conflict in planning would not have happened. For most families working to make everyone happy is always the way to go. Going to the prom for a lot of girls is a dream come true. Make sure when the time is right, on the important events, you are there to support your kids. They are always your first priority.

Always remember the best planned activates and vacations sometimes have to be cancelled or changed. Sometimes, you must sacrifice well thought out plans for insignificant situations of little importance. If your child(ren) are old enough, then if possible allow them to decide how they want to be a part of the family vacation plans. It is important for you to accomplish your goals. If your plans are cancelled once too often, then make it known that you are not going to allow people to walk all over you. Negotiate your arrangement and stick to your plans.

Both parents must do their best to keep all plans on track; however there is that glitch that sometimes comes up that can change or cancel the best made plans. A death in the family or someone gets sick. Perhaps your son's high school baseball team is in the state finals and unexpectedly he is now commitment to play a week after school is out in the state playoffs. This change in plans could be very disappointing and costly to the other parent who expected the child to get on a plane and fly to Arizona for the summer right after school was out. Yes, you could hold your child to his promise to fly to Arizona, however holding your son to a commitment that he has little control over, could cause resentment if you push the issue too far. Be happy for his success and try yourself to make the final game. Remind yourself, time is short. These years, these experiences do not last for long. Show your support: your devotion in all that your children do.

The way both parents must plan access with their child(ren) is simple. Please purchase each year two calendars (One for the wife/partner, one for the husband/partner). Regarding spring break, over-night-weekend stays, or summer vacation write down what goals you have for your child(ren)'s interest or plans.

Write down your work schedule, your time off, who will watch the child(ren) while you are at work if applicable, and then call or meet with the other parent and go over what they too have written down. Work out a schedule that works best for both of you. Since you are making out schedules, try doing the schedule (pencil in if possible beyond 6 months) for the next year. That way, family members will know where they will be, which house the child(ren) will be at each weekend. What time to pick them up, what time to drop them off? Write down their activities, so each parent will know the whereabouts of their child(ren); if they are at soccer practice, or if this is the week mom is out of town, and dad is responsible to take his child(ren) to soccer practice as well as pick them up. The calendar must be very detailed, with notes written down to give information and direction. Each parent must have the same calendar, with all notes and directions included.

One parent should delegate themselves as the calling parent where once a week they call the other parent to remind the other about the following week activities. As the calling parent, you can do it all the time, or you can both decide who will be the caller on a monthly basis, quarterly, or semi-yearly basis. When the caller calls the other parent, (you also can email, text as a way of communicating) go over the weekly logistics to better figure out how to have a smooth transition.

If there is a change on the calendar, the parent who is making the change must be responsible to contact the other parent and inform them about the change; and most importantly, to work out an acceptable agreement. Only in an emergency should you ever make a change in your schedule. You should treat changes the way doctors handle cancellations or changes. If you do not give a 48 hour notice unless there is an emergency, you should expect to be asked for some type of concession. If you change plans a lot, then a session with a mediator might be in order. Changing plans upsets your child(ren) and everyone around them. It is your responsibility to be where you are supposed to be on time and ready to participate in the event that you have planned. Except for emergencies, there should never be changes in your plans. You should expect the same type of behavior from your spouse/partner.

A FEW QUESTIONS AND SUGGESTIONS REGARDING ACCESS DURING SCHOOL YEAR.

IMPORTANT NOTE TO PARENTS:
THE SUGGESTIONS THAT ARE IN THIS PROGRAM ARE THOUGHT OUT SUGGESTIONS THAT HAVE BEEN IMPLEMENTED BY THOUSANDS OF PEOPLE WHO HAVE TAKEN OUR PROGRAM. FOR SOME, THE INFORMATION WE ARE GIVING MAY NOT BE WHAT THE JUDGE (THE COURTS) OR YOUR ATTORNEY WILL ADVISE YOU TO DO. AT ALL TIMES IF A JUDGE ORDERS YOU TO NOT DO SOMETHING THAT WE HAVE SUGGESTED, THEN THAT IS WHAT YOU ARE REQUIRED TO DO. HERE IS AN EXAMPLE, LET'S SAY THE JUDGE FORBIDS YOU TO GO ANYWHERE NEAR YOUR CHILD(REN). YOU ARE ONLY ALLOWED TO SEE THEM ON SUPERVISED VISITATION. HOWEVER IN THE NEXT CHAPTER, WE ARE SUGGESTING IDEAS ON HOW TO HANDLE WORKING WITH YOUR CHILD(REN)'S SCHOOL AND THEIR TEACHERS. IF A JUDGE SAYS YOU CANNOT DO THE ITEMS WE HAVE SUGGESTED, THEN YOU MUST FOLLOW THOSE ORDERS THE JUDGE GAVE

YOU AND NOT GO TO THE SCHOOL OR HAVE ANY CONTACT WITH YOUR CHILD(REN), THEIR SCHOOL, OR THEIR TEACHER WITHOUT WRITTEN PERMISSION FROM THE COURTS. THIS NOT ONLY PERTAINS TO THIS CHAPTER, BUT IS REQUIRED FOR THE ENTIRE PROGRAM.

WHEN THOSE FUN DAYS OF SUMMER ARE OVER AND THE KIDS ARE ENTHUSIASTICALLY ANTICIPATING THE FIRST DAY OF SCHOOL, SOME POINTS SHOULD BE COVERED TO KEEP BOTH PARENTS INFORMED.

Make sure the school has both parent's emergency information and permission for both parents (if allowed by the courts) to pick up their child(ren). Both parents in most cases should be allowed access to all school records.

On the first day of school, both parents might want to be at the bus stop or go together to meet the teacher. If that is not possible, write an informative brief note for your child(ren) to take to school to notify the teacher that your child(ren) has two homes; give the teacher both addresses. If applicable let the teacher as well as the school administrative office know that both of you want to have an active role in your child(ren)'s school work, as well as on occasion you might want to get involved with participating as a volunteer in school events and activities.

It is important that report cards, any correspondence regarding your child(ren), any homework assignment, any discipline report, any absentee report, goes to both parents. This can be done by email if applicable. Make sure the mode of communication between school and parents is agreed upon by both parent's. If the teacher and or school develop the mode of communication between households, inform your spouse/partner how the school and teacher wish to proceed. Make sure the school is aware that any email/correspondence that goes to one parent must go to both parents.

If the teacher sends a newsletter home or any item of interest about what the school is doing, open house, school PTA, PTO meetings, both parents need to be notified. If a parent is requested to schedule an appointment with the school or the teacher, both parents need to be notified. The parent that is requesting the meeting must, in writing, inform the other parent what date and time the meeting will take place as well as why the meeting has been arranged. The parent, who has arranged the meeting, should give adequate notice to the other parent, so they have time to arrange their schedule.

LIVING IN CLOSE PROXIMITY TO YOUR CHILD(REN)'S SCHOOL

We suggest if possible, when one parent moves out, they move within the school district where their child(ren) are going to school already. It is so much easier for all concerned that on Monday morning; the kids have an option (if applicable) to get on a school bus that transports within the same school system. Some benefits to living close to one another is the child(ren) may be able to walk to and from school from both of the home's they live in. Your child(ren)'s friends are the same friends they play with at home and at school. Most importantly, both parents are connected to the same neighborhood. The school feels comfortable calling either parent to come pick up a sick child when both parents live close to the school. Think about it, who do you think the school will call in a time of need? Security word custody note word and page number. The father who lives down the street, or the mother who lives 30 minutes away from the school? Lastly it is so much easier when your child knows you are within minutes of their call, or when you have custody of your children, they will only have to be driven a few minutes to see you or the other parent. Your child's friends can stay overnight and their parents can conveniently pick up the child that slept over the following morning. The library and all resources are conveniently in close proximity to your family's homes, the pool, sports practice; scout and social club meetings; going to the school or high school events does not have to take an hour of travel time. These are some of the reasons you might want to check out living close to your spouse/partner and your kids.

Yes, there are drawbacks to living so close to your spouse/partner, however the advantages verses the disadvantages far out way living across town when it comes to being close to your kids.

First and foremost, child support for most does not include the cost of extra-curricular activities. These costs are extra and go over and beyond child support. Parent's say, I pay support, take the cost of the activity out of my support. Usually, it does not work that way. Saying to your wife/husband, "I give you child support that is enough," does not cut it. Child support does not pay for any extra item your child(ren) might need. Both spouses/partners need to budget for these costs, because for most, if your child(ren) are busy in out-of–school activities, the costs can be substantial. Even if the activity is done within the school confines, there most likely will be some cost that relates to the activity. For example, if your teen is in football, they might be required to have a sports physical, buy their own shoes, a cup, and perhaps health or injury insurance.

WORKBOOK QUESTIONS,

(11-1) What activities do your child(ren) participate in?

_____

(11-2) How much will the activities cost per month? Per year?

_____

(11-3) How will the extra cost be paid?

_____

SCHOOL, PUBLIC OR PRIVATE:

(11-4) What do kids need when it comes to preparing for the school year and who should pay?

_____

(11-5) What school public or private will your child(ren) go to?

_____

(11-6) If private school, who will pay for the tuition?

_____

(11-7) Who will pay next year and what amount?

_____

(11-8) Who will take the child(ren) to school?

_____

(11-9) Who will bring them home?

_____

(11-10) Both parties try to agree on what school is the best for your child(ren) and who will pay for the tuition. Please use the mediation steps used in the mediation segment video.

_____

(11-11) Who will pay for books and school supplies?

_____

(11-12) Are your child(ren) allowed to be involved with extra-curricular activities?

(11-13) Who will pick the child(ren) up from these activities? _____ Who takes them to the activities? _____. If the child is a teenager, can their friends pick them up? What is the rule about driving with other teens in a car?

Notes:

Chapter 12 - A Healthy Divorce - From Adolescents To Becoming A Teenager

WORKBOOK QUESTIONS,

(12-1) How to work together when the child(ren) are caught in the middle, or the child(ren) are manipulating you?

(12-2) If you say no to an idea or problem, and the other parent says yes; how will both of you handle this situation?

(12-3) If the child(ren)'s grades go down, what do you do?

(12-4) Who picks the child(ren) up from school or event if the child(ren) gets sick?

(12-5) Who will watch them until they go back to school?

(12-6) Who buys your child(ren)'s clothes?

(12-7) Who pays for the clothes?

_____

(12-8) Who buys the extra-curricular uniform, musical instrument?

_____

(12-9) Who pays for tutoring, going on field trips, extra costs?

_____

(12-10) If your child is old enough, who will teach them how to drive? Will they be given a car to drive back and forth to school? Who will pay for the car? Who will pay for insurance on the car? Who will pay to maintain/repair the car? Who will establish the rules for use of the car; can they have anyone in the car with them? Are they allowed to talk on the phone/text when driving? When you call them, should they talk to you while they are driving? How far can they go with the car?

_____

(12-11) Have you planned for college? Are you in a college plan? Who will pay for the plan? How will it be set up?

_____

(12-12) Who pays for the actives and extra cost that go along with the sport/extra circular activities?

_____

(12-13) Continuing or beginning lessons for child(ren): who and how are the lessons going to be paid for?

_____

(12-14) Who will drive them to lessons? _____ Who will drive them home? _____

(12-15) Remedial help and necessary tutoring for the child(ren): who and how will this help be paid for?

_____

(12-16) Who will drive them to tutoring? _____ Who will drive them home? _____

(12-17) Who will pay FOR EXPENSES, when child(ren) are in school and what amount? WHO WILL PAY FOR COLLEGE OR SCHOOL AFTER HIGH SCHOOL? Will they go to a local college or is out-of-state college acceptable? Who will pay for room and board?

_____

_____

Do you have professional accountants or C.P.A.'s helping your with your Tax Issues?

_____

_____

NOTES:

Chapter 13 - A Healthy Divorce - I.R.S. Tax Credit

AT THIS POINT ANY ARRANGEMENT YOU MAKE IS NEGOTIABLE. IF BOTH OF YOU CLAIM THE CHILD(REN), IRS COULD LOOK AT THIS SITUATION AS FOLLOWS:

Understanding the tax code is difficult. Since it changes each year a call to your accountant at this point is necessary so you may first understand how to best get the most out of allowed deductions, as well as what your rights are as a taxpayer and how the tax laws work for or against you.

TAX FILING, EXEMPTIONS, AND LIABILITY (AS OF 2013) GENERAL RULE FOR TAX EXEMPTIONS FOR CHILD(REN):

The code provides that a custodial parent after a divorce is entitled to the dependency exemption for his or her child(ren) even though the non-custodial parent pays more than half the support for the child(ren). There are exceptions to this general rule, so be sure to talk to your accountant prior to filing.

The parent having "custody" according to the divorce decree or written separation agreement is defined as the custodial parent. If the decree or agreement doesn't clearly delineate who has custody, or if the question of custody is in dispute on the last day of the year, the custodial parent is the one who had physical custody of the child(ren) for the greater portion of the calendar year Reg.§1.152-4(b)

This is a general guide, and not to be looked at as fact. There are exemptions to the rule, and guidelines that help define all the variables that go into the equation on how to establish who has the right to claim the child(ren).

To understand the tax code better regarding tax exemptions, here is a true story on how the courts ruled on one family's court battle regarding "Who gets to claim the child(ren)?"

Jennifer Rogers and. William Lautenberger divorced in 1993. Their custody order provided for joint custody of their daughter Diana, with physical custody split equally between them on a weekly basis. On their 1998 federal income tax returns, both claimed Diana age 14, as a dependent and both claimed the child(ren) tax credit. Mr. Lautenberg from a previous marriage had other child(ren) that will also be mentioned in the evidence that he will later submit.

The key in this case is custody. In the case of divorced parents, if the parents together provide more than 50% of the child(ren)'s support, then the dependency exemption will go to the parent who has custody for more than 50% of the year. The IRS Regulations state "In the event of so-called 'split' custody... custody will be deemed to be with the parent who has the physical custody of the child(ren) for the greater portion of the calendar year" (Beg. §1.152-4(b))

Mr. Lautenberger claimed he had custody for 187 days of the year due to a vacation he took with Diana. He furnished a chart listing the days Diana was with him and the days she was with Ms. Rogers. He also furnished two diaries in support of his claim. The diaries had numbers "0", "2", or "4" on the first page of each week indicating how many child(ren) were with him that week, but did not indicate which child(ren) the numbers referred to nor which child(ren) lived with him on any particular day of the week.

Ms. Rogers testified that they shared custody "50/50" and she did not keep track of every minute that Diana was with either of them. She also stated that she picked Diana up from school and activities when she was sick, let her go on vacation with her father, and that Diana often stopped at her house after school. She further stated that the shared custody arrangement is for Diana's benefit, not to be manipulated for a tax exemption.

The Tax Court determined that Mr. Lautenberger's testimony and evidence was unconvincing while Ms. Roger's testimony was convincing. As such, the Court determined Diana spent equal time with each parent; therefore neither had physical custody for more than 50% or the year. As such, neither parent is allowed the dependency exemption or the child(ren) tax credit for 1998. Jennifer A. Rogers and William Lautenberger, T.C Summary Opinion 2002-41

SOMETIMES IT DOES NOT PAY TO GO TO COURT AND NOT NEGOTIATE ISSUES AMONG YOURSELF AND YOUR SPOUSE/PARTNER.

ONE OTHER ITEM THAT COULD BE OF INTEREST TO YOU AS FAR AS CHILD(REN) AND IRS ISSUES.

TAX CREDIT REGARDING CHILD CARE COSTS

Code §21(a) allows certain taxpayers to claim a tax-credit equal to from 20% to 30% of certain employment-related dependent care expenses. The credit is available to taxpayers who maintain a household that includes one or more dependents who are either below the age of 13 or incapable of caring for themselves. The credit applies to expenses of household services and care for dependents that enable the taxpayer to be gainfully employed. In divorce, this credit is available only to the parent who has custody for a greater portion of the year.

THERE ARE SO MANY TAX QUESTIONS WE HAVE NOT COVERED.

Am I entitled to alimony, who gets the marital home, and if we agree to allow my spouse to keep the home, who gets to claim the interest on the mortgage, the property tax? Who gets the vacation home or investment property? Will there be capital gains/losses and if so who is responsible to pay for these costs? What about retirement? Am I entitled to ½ of my spouse/partners 401 retirements? Good accountants who understand retirement plans and investments can help establish for both parties your best financial options not only for during and after the divorce, but for both of your financial futures. It is worth spending a few dollars to get good advice. For most, you work hard for your money. Don't throw money away to find a quick fix. Count on an expert to advise you, to make the best decision. If you cannot agree on who should advise you; choose separate accountants, give both accountants the same information, and see what they each come up with. If necessary allow both accountants to come together to work out the best financial plan for the both of you. Take action today to protect your family tomorrow.

WORKBOOK QUESTIONS,

(13-1) Who gets the child(ren) tax credit?

_____

(13-2) When you need to determine if you can claim your child(ren); how do you establish custody?

_____

(13-3) Can you claim Child Care Tax Credit?

_____

Chapter 14 - A Healthy Divorce - Transporting Children, Costs Of Schools, Who Pays, Who Chooses School? Spouse And Sharing Children.

SUGGESTIONS AND IDEAS TO THINK ABOUT REGARDING TRANSPORTING THE CHILD(REN).

Several parents throughout this course have made the point that if my spouse wants to see the kids then they can come and pick them up and bring them back. We hear, "It is not my job to transport. I simply am not going to do it." This is a mutual task that both parents need to be involved in. If you have the child(ren), it is your responsibility to get the child(ren) to the other parents home; this includes long distance travel. If your spouse lives two thousand miles away, most likely in conversation, the question has come up, "Who will pay for the transportation?" And if your child(ren) are young, "Who is responsible to make sure the child(ren) has adequate supervision while traveling?" Unless otherwise court ordered, the parent who currently has the kids in their custody (not who has custody) is responsibility to transport the child(ren) to the airport or to the other parent's residence.

As you develop your parenting plan it is important to make sure each parent is sharing the responsibility of transportation. Prior to finalizing your divorce this issue should be addressed and decided. A workable solution could be to meet half way. This will save both parents time and sometimes money when traveling back and forth. Be prompt and if you say you will be at your agreed to pick-up-point at four in the afternoon, make sure you are at the point of contact on time. Another alternative is taking turns. One parent transports the kids and takes the child(ren) to the other parent's home, then that parent returns the child(ren) to the other household.

Something for you to think about. It may put a lot of stress on the child(ren), as well as the parent who must travel to and from their house when the kid's live four or more hours away. When child(ren) spend the majority or a good part of their free time in the backseat of a vehicle traveling on weekends to one parents home and then back home again, both parents must ask themselves, if this is being fair to all concerned? Instead try having a long weekend at a hotel in the same city where the other spouse lives. Take a mini weekend trip and visit a state park that is close to the child(ren)'s other home. Work creatively with the other parent to come up with better solutions. Perhaps spending less time during school days with your child(ren) and more time together on holidays and summer vacation, might be easier on the child(ren)/family. Maybe the child(ren) could go to school one year at the residence of the father and one year at the residence of the mother. Living in the middle, where it is a long way to go for a weekend and to close to get on a plane can be a problem. The cost of transportation can be problematic. It is not cheap, to transport child(ren), especially long distance. The bottom line is that your child(ren) love you both, and they want to be a part of your life. Working towards your child(ren)'s desires as well as their need to be loved by both parents is very important for their development.

Work hard in developing an access plan between you and your spouse. When possible, let the child(ren) have a say on how they would like to develop their plan to be with both parents. Write your plan down and incorporate it into your parenting plan. This plan will eventually become part of your divorce decree; as well as a legal document. Take it serious as it is intended to be. If you cannot conform to what you agree to, do not sign the agreement. Having said that, you still need to come up with a plan. Learn to negotiate, mediate your plan so it works to protect you, your spouse, and your child(ren). Remember, anything you discuss and agree on, must be in writing. Take the time to make a good plan that will stand the test of time.

Who will be in charge of picking the daycare/school or will it be a mutual decision? Who will pay for child(ren) care/tuition for private school?

WORKBOOK QUESTIONS,
(14-1) How are you going to handle transportation between the two households? PLEASE DETAIL.

Chapter 15 - A Healthy Divorce - How Do You Stay Connected With Your Spouse/Partner When You Have The Children? Children Need To Know Their Grandparents.

Many parents do not want to communicate with their spouse when they have their child(ren). However your thoughts on that idea will be different if the shoe is on the other foot. Communicating is a two-way street. If you are on vacation, in or out of town encourage your kids to call the other parent once a day. If you are on vacation, give your itinerary to the other parent; so they know where their kids are vacationing and how to get a hold of you in an emergency. If you are going to be late arriving at your destination, call the other parent to inform them that you have been detained. Security word support note word and page number. A quick call can relieve thoughts that their child(ren) could be in danger. Give access to your kids to call the other parent as often as they feel necessary. Use email and other ways to communicate with your spouse. Never look at your child(ren), as your possession. They are a gift. Share that gift with your spouse and other members of her/his family especially grandparents. When doing your parenting plans, have you included weekends and summer activities with both grandparents and other members of the family? Make sure you include your family in your child(ren) lives. Family especially grandparents provides your child(ren) with their history. Child(ren) need to know their family's history; where they came from, so they will have a better understanding on where they are going.

WORKBOOK QUESTIONS,

(15-1) How do you stay connected to your spouse when you have the child(ren)?

_____

_____

_____

_____

(15-2) What activities do I have planned with both sets of grandparents or family members?

_____

_____

_____

_____

Chapter 16 - A Healthy Divorce - Traveling Out Of State Or Country?

For most people traveling with your entire family is both educational and fun for all. Before, when you were married or living together you thought nothing about getting on a plane with your kids and going to see Grandma in Germany so why now is it a problem? Divorce brings on so many challenging and awkward, sticky moments. Taking your child(ren) out of the country, even out of the state might be frightful to the other parent. Will my child(ren) be safe, will they bring the child(ren) back to the states? Surely if you were in your spouse's shoes, you most likely would think the same thing. Therefore, during a divorce process, most attorneys would frown when consulted about their client's child(ren) being taken out of the country or state. If it is so important for your child(ren) to see their relatives that live a long distance away, perhaps the relatives could visit you until the divorce is over. Once that phase is over, most parents knowing their rights regarding their child(ren) might feel better about a long extended stay away from the child(ren). Time usually cures bad thoughts, as well as feelings. However if you want your child(ren) to leave the state or country, make sure that process is written into your divorce decree. You will want a judge to sanction your taking your child(ren) outside the country or state and agree with you that it is in the best interest of the child(ren).

WORKBOOK QUESTIONS,

(16-1) What are your feelings about your spouse taking your child(ren) out of the state or country?

_____
_____
_____
_____

(16-2) When a major life event happens to your spouse, what should be your position as an ex. (spouse/partner)?

_____
_____
_____
_____

NOTES:

_____
_____
_____

Chapter 17 - A Healthy Divorce - After Divorce, When Family Still Counts.

Every life at times has crises. A family member of your ex. is suddenly sick or a death occurs in their immediate family. What is your role? Total support, suppress all of your past anger; understand and feel compassion for your spouse and your child(ren)'s sadness. Especially for your child(ren) if nothing else, do your best to rise to the occasion.

Go to your spouse, ask if there is anything you can do, and be supportive. Get the child(ren) ready for a week family stay. Make reservations to transport the child(ren) to the place where they will be staying, make sure they understand what is going on and that they are loved; if they are old enough, explain to them the grief process. Give them as much time as they need with their other parent as well as his/her family. Try to work through the pain, hurt and your own sorrow to console your child(ren). Most of all cooperate and put your best foot forward. Show your child(ren) how strong you have become in time of crisis. Give them space and time to grieve. Prepare to answer their questions when they return home. Remember even if you did not get along with your late in-laws, your child(ren) most likely loved them. Show the utmost respect for your spouse's family and your child(ren)'s relatives.

Things happen in life that are unexpected, hard to handle, and disappointing. A wife can't make it on her own, so she and the child(ren) have nowhere else to go; but to move back with her parents three thousand miles away. A brother of your ex-spouse opens a restaurant in another state and offers a job to your ex-husband. Your ex and her new husband want to begin a new life in Asia learning how to speak the language. These things happen. What now? Prior to getting a divorce, it is essential to do a declaration of understanding on how you intend to handle any major life changes or lifestyle changes regarding you, your spouse, or your child(ren). You can agree to grant their request, however the child(ren) follow the same schedule as before. You can agree to go to mediation, arbitration, or court to resolve these issues. You can agree that after the divorce, until the child(ren) are 18 years of age they will live only in the state where they currently reside, in the county where they go to school period; unless in writing both parents/partners agree on the terms of the agreement / contract. This is your divorce, your contract. You can structure/write the terms of your divorce/separation within the statue of the law, anyway both you and your husband/wife sees fit.

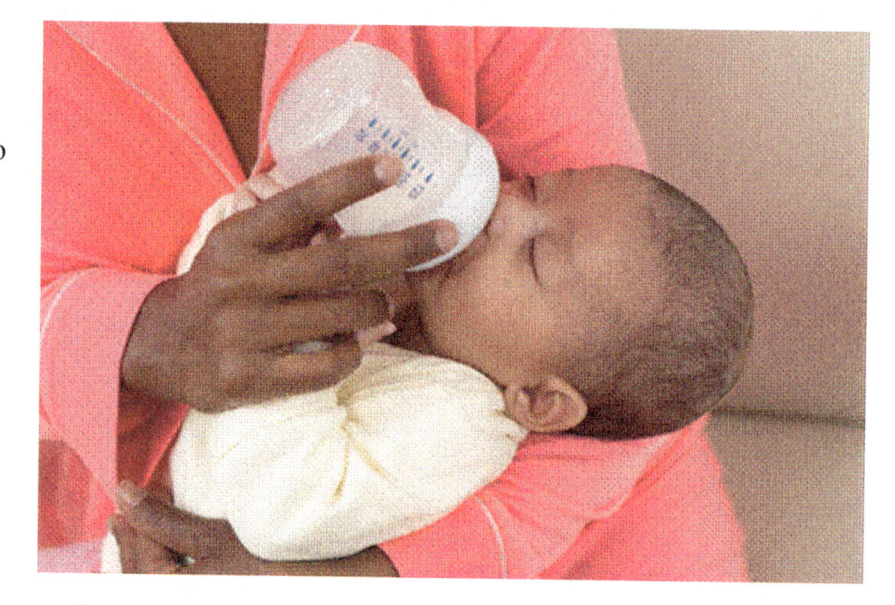

WORKBOOK QUESTIONS,

(17-1) In your divorce decree, add to your parenting plan a section on what to do when major life events happen? How will you handle a major life event when a crisis happens to your spouse/partner?

(17-2) What options are there if your spouse/partner or you have a major life change?

(17-3) What agreement would you write, regarding major lifestyle changes or events?

Notes:

Chapter 18 - A Healthy Divorce - Child Support Guidelines/Child Support Amounts

A child support order tells the parents what they must do to support their child(ren). Enforcing child support orders means getting the parent(s) to do what the order says.

The amount of child support is based on guidelines defined by state statues. Child support guidelines are standards used to figure out the support needed for the child(ren) and the amount a parent is required to pay. Guidelines help make sure support amounts are fair. Every state has guidelines, but they may be different in each state.

These guidelines are used the first time child support is ordered and every time the child support amount changes. They are also used to review the order to see if the support amount should be changed.

State child support guidelines could consider:

- The income of both parents
- The child(ren)'s health care and child care costs
- The standard needs for the child(ren). A list of support amounts based on the child(ren)'s age and net income of the parents usually are considerations based on the "standard needs table".

The court or agency establishing support must use these guidelines to decide the amount of child support that will go in a support order. In special circumstances, support amounts can be higher or lower than the guideline amounts. For example, a judge may consider a child's high medical expenses as a reason to change the support amount. In most cases, judges have to give written reasons why support amounts are different from guideline amounts.

You can get an estimate of child support amounts by going to your state's Child Support Calculator. The calculator will take the information you put in and give you an estimate of your child support amount. This estimate is for informational purposes only. A court or agency may look at factors that are not included in your estimate.

Notes about Child Support:

Chapter 19 - A Healthy Divorce - Health And Dental Care For Children: Insurance And Sharing Costs Not Covered By Insurance.

In some states this is an area where couples getting divorced may negotiate. If you have great insurance, you might want to negotiate your insurance coverage for more child support or other areas that you see as a concern. If your company pays for insurance and dental care and your spouse's company does not pay any benefits, you have a negotiating tool.

Some states look at health insurance and child care when determining child support. Looking at who pays these costs; the amount of child support may be increased or decreased, based on who and how much one parent pays regarding health insurance and child care.

Since insurance rules and regulations as of 2014 has change, it is important that you look at all sides of your insurance coverage, your spouse/partners coverage and find which one will be the best policy for your family, as well as what premium you can best afford. Take into consideration, co-pays, who is going to pay. Who will pay the bill, for areas like eye care; if neither of you are covered by this type of insurance policy? Make sure both of you have the right to give permission for your child to received medical care and extended care should an emergency arise. Make sure both parents have all the child(ren)'s insurance cards, medical, and vaccination records.

Notes about Health and Dental Coverage:

Chapter 20 - A Healthy Divorce - Handling Religious Education, How Do Courts Decide Which Religion The Child(ren) Should Follow When Parents Of Different Religions Separate?

Deciding whose religion the child(ren) should follow after a divorce or separation can often be a difficult and contentious question to answer. Increasingly parents of different faiths marry and have children. When these parents get divorced, it is often up to the courts to decide which religion the child(ren) should follow. Observing courts all around the country, there is not a uniform standard that individual courts follow when answering difficult questions regarding religion.

BEST INTEREST OF THE CHILD(REN) OR THE RIGHTS OF THE PARENTS.

When courts are asked to answer the question of what religion the child(ren) should follow after a separation or divorce, they often balance two competing interests, the best interests of the child(ren), and the rights of the parents. Security word school note word and page number. On one side, courts routinely answer questions about what is in the best interests of a child(ren) and have become quite proficient with these types of issues.

On the other hand, the First Amendment of the United States Constitution protects the parents' freedom of religion as well as their right to raise their child(ren) under the religion of their choosing.

Often, in a case where a court must make a decision about a child's religious upbringing, one parent will argue that raising the child(ren) under the other parent's religion will put the welfare of the child(ren) in danger. When faced with this question, the court must weigh the benefits and costs of one parent's First Amendment rights versus the best interests of the child(ren).

CHILD(REN) CUSTODY AND RELIGIOUS LAW IN DIFFERENT CASES/STATES

In general, there is not a national standard for cases involving the religious upbringing of a child(ren) after a divorce. Because of this, the law varies from state to state. However, most state courts will generally apply one of the following standards when ruling in a child(ren) custody and religion case:

- **Actual or substantial harm standard.** When a court follows this standard, the court will restrict a parent's First Amendment right to raise their child(ren) under the religion of their choosing only if that parent's religious practice causes actual or substantial harm to the child(ren).
- **Risk of harm standard.** When a court follows this standard, the court will only restrict a parent's First Amendment right to raise their child(ren) under the religion of their choosing if a parent's religious practice may cause harm to the child(ren).
- **No harm standard.** When a court follows this standard, the court does not consider any actual or potential harm to the child(ren). Instead, the parent that has been granted custody of the child(ren) gets to choose which religion the child(ren) will follow. If the custodial parent objects to the non-custodial parent's wishes for the religion of the child(ren), the court will side with the custodial parent.

ACTUAL AND SUBSTANTIAL HARM/CASE LAW

Under this standard, a court will only restrict a parent's First Amendment right to raise their child(ren) under a religion of their choosing when the other parent can prove that those religious activities cause actual or substantial harm to the child(ren). There are many states that follow this standard including California, Colorado, Florida, Idaho, Indiana, Iowa, Maryland, Massachusetts, Montana, Nebraska, New Jersey, New York, North Dakota, Ohio, Rhode Island, Utah, Vermont, and Washington.

What follows are a list of cases that show how the actual or substantial harm standard was applied to a variety of situations. You should keep in mind that even if you find a case that you think may apply to your situation, if the case did not take place in your state, your state's courts may not apply the law in the same way. Indeed, courts in the same states do not always apply the same law in a uniform manner.

Munoz v. Munoz -- This case ruled that exposing children to two different religions does not, in itself, cause harm to the children.

In **Munoz v. Munoz**, Washington State's highest court had to decide whether exposing a child(ren) to two different religions in itself caused harm to the child(ren). In this case, the divorce court awarded sole custody of the children to the mother, who was Mormon. After the custody award, the mother asked the court to prevent the father, who was Catholic, from exposing the children to his own faith. However, the mother did not provide any evidence or likely arguments that exposing the children to both the Mormon and Catholic faiths would harm the children, either physically or mentally. Because of this, the Washington State Supreme Court ruled that exposing children to two different religions does not automatically harm the children and decided not to curtail the father's First Amendment rights to raise his children under his faith.

Pater v. Pater -- This case ruled that religious customs are not harmful unless proven otherwise.

In **Pater v. Pater**, the Ohio Supreme Court overruled a lower court decision that had switched the custody award from the mother to the father. The lower court had decided that way because the mother, who originally had sole custody, was a Jehovah's Witness and had the children practicing her faith. Under the mother's faith, the children could not celebrate any holidays, be friends with anyone outside of the religion, salute the American flag or sing the national anthem. The lower court decided that this was harmful to the children.

However, the Ohio Supreme Court reversed this decision and took sole custody away from the Catholic father. In doing so, the court ruled that religious customs that diminish a child(ren)'s social activities are not harmful (even if the customs separate the child(ren) from his or her peers or preach against standards of the community), unless it can be proven that the customs directly cause physical or mental harm to the child(ren). Here, the Ohio Supreme Court did not see any evidence of direct physical or mental harm.

Kendall v. Kendall -- This cased ruled that physical acts and verbal threats were enough to justify an intervention of a parent's First Amendment rights.

In **Kendall v. Kendall**, the Massachusetts Supreme Court was dealing with a case that involved an Orthodox Jewish mother and a Catholic father. When the couple was first married, they agreed to raise their children under the Jewish faith. After the mother filed for divorce, the father made threats to his son. These threats included the threat to cut off his son's religions clothing unless he tucked them into his pants as well as a threat to cut off his sons "payes" (the curls in the hair that are normally worn by Orthodox Jewish men). In addition, the father told his children that anyone outside of his Catholic faith was damned to go to hell.

The mother challenged the father's First Amendment rights based on testimony from a doctor that the father's threats caused mental and emotional harm to the children. Because of the evidence that was presented, the court prohibited the father from talking to his children about his faith and also banned him from shaving off his son's "payes". In addition, the church barred him from studying the Bible with his children and praying with them if those activities would tend to get the children to reject the Orthodox Jewish faith or cause emotional distress.

RISKS AND HARM

There are a few states, including Minnesota, Montana, North Carolina, and Pennsylvania, which follow the risk of harm standard instead of applying the actual or substantial harm standard. Courts that follow the risk of harm standard only require that the parent challenging the other parent's First Amendment right show that there is a risk of harm instead of showing actual or substantial harm.

MacLagan v. Klein -- This case ruled on the risk of harm standard.

In **MacLagan v. Klein**, a North Carolina state court was faced with a case where the father of a child wanted to stop the mother from changing their daughter's faith. When the couple was first married, they agreed to raise their children under the father's Jewish faith. When the couple divorce, the mother began bringing their daughter to a Methodist church. The father did not agree with this decision and asked the court to allow him to have full control of his daughter's religious upbringing. Applying the risk of harm standard, the court found that the daughter had identified herself with the Jewish faith since the age of three and that exposing her to the Methodist faith may cause her emotional harm. Because of this, the court agreed with the father and granted him sole control over his daughter's religious education.

You may have noticed the big difference between the MacLagan case and the Munoz case. The two cases had very similar facts that the courts looked at, but came out with two very different outcomes. The difference in outcomes is based on the fact that the two courts applied very different standards to their decision making process.

NO HARM

There are a few states, including Arkansas and Wisconsin, which do not look at any harms, whether real or a risk, to children and instead defer to the parent with custody of the child(ren). In general, in states that follow the no harm standard, the parent that has sole legal custody over the child(ren) has the sole right to decide on the religious education of the child(ren). If a dispute arises between the custodial parent and the non-custodial parent, the court will generally decide to side with the custodial parent. In general, the courts that decide this way that the decision is in the best interests of the child(ren) and that any restrictions on the non-custodial parent's First Amendment rights is small because the only time the rights are curtailed is when the parent is with the child(ren).

If both parents have been granted legal custody of the child(ren), both parents are generally allowed to give the child(ren) their own religious education.

Johns v. Johns -- The court ruled that the parent with legal custody gets to decide.

In **Johns v. Johns**, an Arkansas state court agreed with the mother who had both legal and physical custody of the children. In this case, the court was faced with a problem where the mother of the children refused to allow the father his visitation time because he did not take the kids to church or Sunday school when he was supposed to. The father challenged this action, but the mother prevailed in court because she was the custodial parent and the court agreed with her and ordered that the father must take the children to church and Sunday school.

Zummo v. Zummo -- The court ruled that joint legal custody can mean two religions.

In **Zummo v. Zummo**, the court was faced with problem where both parents shared legal custody of the children but disagreed on which religious upbringing their children should take part in. To put a stop to the problem, the court ordered that the father needs to take his children to Jewish services (the mother's religion), but was also allowed to bring his children to Catholic services as well (his religion). The court rationalized that because both parents shared legal custody, they both had the right to provide their children with their own religions education.

SOME STATES CAN USE MORE THAN ONE STANDARD

You should be aware that in some states, like Montana and Pennsylvania, courts often use different standards. For instance, one court in Montana could use the actual or substantial harm standard while another court in the same building may decide to apply the risk of harm or no harm standard.

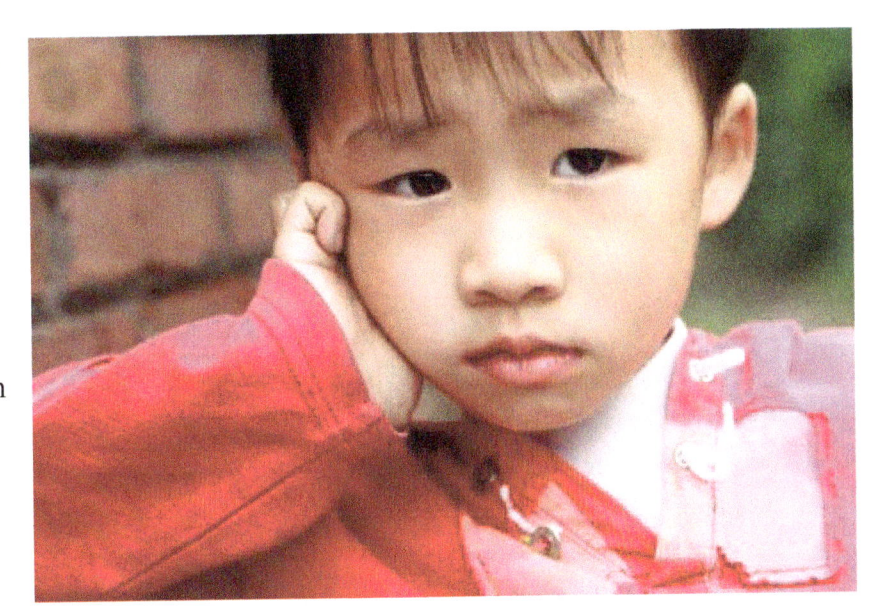

CHILD(REN) CUSTODY AND PARENTING AGREEMENT

Courts will often take parenting agreements into account in their decisions if parents have made some sort of written or oral parenting agreement where they decide how to handle a child(ren)'s religions upbringing. However, you should keep in mind that if you and your spouse have not followed the agreement, you should not expect the court to give it too much weight. As well, many courts will not give weight to any agreements that take into account which religion a child(ren) will follow in the event that the parents separate or divorce. Here are some of the reasons that courts give:

The agreement is not detailed enough. Generally speaking, many parents do not think a parenting agreement regarding child(ren) and religion is very important and because of this they are often informal and vague. As an example, most agreements do not take into account the degree of religious education that the child(ren) will receive (such as whether or not the child(ren) will attend Sunday school or how often the child(ren) will attend religious services) and merely specify which faith a child(ren) will follow.

The agreement was oral. Like oral contracts for almost anything else, parties to an oral parenting agreement will often have different accounts of just what exactly the agreement was. As well, just like almost all other oral contracts, a court will not enforce an oral parenting agreement if the court cannot determine exactly what was agreed.

The agreement is very old. Many young couples that get married often wait a while before having child(ren). If the couple made a parenting agreement a long time before they had their first child(ren), or the agreement is old for any other reasons, a court may not lend that much weight to it.

Courts do not like to diminish First Amendment or parenting rights. Because of their importance, courts do not generally like to stomp down on the parenting or First Amendment rights of parents. In addition, courts do not generally like to issue orders that enforce prior-made parenting agreements as this can lead to excessive governmental involvement in the private lives of parents.

It is important to realize that not all courts dislike parenting agreements that discuss the religious upbringing of children. For example, in Wilson v. Wilson, an Indiana court ruled that a divorce agreement that contained terms regarding the religious education of the children was binding on the parents.

To sum up, if you think that you would like to have a parenting agreement that involves the religious education of your child(ren), you should make sure that the agreement is very detailed, in writing and not more than a few years old.

SUMMARIZE

If you've learned anything from this, it should be that the outcome of your case will depend greatly on the state that you filed your case in. In addition, you should also realize that because there is no uniform national law that deals with this situation, the laws of your state could change at any time. Because of this, it is almost always better for you and the other parent to try to resolve any issues regarding child(ren) custody and religion outside of court.

If you fear that your child(ren) may be harmed, or is already being harmed by the religious activities of the other parent, you should try to take your child(ren) to a mental health professional. By bringing in experts, you may quiet your own fears by finding out that there are no risks of harm, or if there is harm, you will have evidence to support your case should you decide to go to court.

Statistics show us if you do end up going to court to resolve a situation involving child(ren) custody and religion, you should keep in mind that you have the best chance of success if you have sole or joint legal custody.

Chapter 21 - A Healthy Divorce - Yearly Access Plan

Culminating all that we have gone over, then times it by each year that both you and your spouse remain alive to enjoy your child(ren). Co-Parenting starts today. It never ends. You will always be a co-parent to your child(ren). You will hopefully experience their first recital, high school prom, college graduation, they getting married, having your forth grandchild, so on and so forth. Co-Parenting is life, and it works for most. Each year agree to meet, be prepared. Your kids have grown, found new interests, aspired to new goals. Your job together is to provide for your child(ren) so they can meet their goals one phase at a time. Your organization and co-parenting skills will take your child(ren) to every level of development that you see they can achieve. Positive goals and a demand for both parents to be the best parent will allow your child(ren) to obtain goals that you never thought possible. When your child(ren) are in middle school, start talking about college, take them to local colleges and show them their future. In high school, have them start looking at colleges, go to college orientations and allow your child(ren) to participate in activities that prepare them for college. By their junior year, make sure you have a check list that has been completed focusing on the demand most colleges put on perspectives as they scout, looking for that exceptional student to enter their school. Work together and focus on what is really important for your child(ren) and work towards obtaining their goals. Above all, remember who your child(ren) looks up to is you. Be the role model you want your child(ren) to be. If you want them to have fun all their life, show them a good time. If you want them to succeed, show them responsibility and truth. If you want them to love and learn how to love, show them respect, trust, loyalty, and tenderness. If you want them to be successful, you must show them what success is. If you want them to be a looser…"That will never happen, after all they are your children". We wish you luck with your co-parenting skills. We wish you the best of success to you and your family.

IF YOU HAVE TRIED CO-PARENTING AND IT HAS FAILED, TRY SOLUTIONS FOR DIVORCING PARENTS IN HIGH CONFLICT "PARALLEL PARENTING"

If Co-Parenting is not for you or your spouse/partner, Parallel Parenting and it's method of training could be. Parallel Parenting is "life changing" and could "fill in the gap"; when parents are left without any type of consistent program to base their parenting relationship on. Please note, that this is not a comparison to other trainings in mediation, collaboration, or other high conflict programs. It is a process, a tool used in many divorce cases where educators should be aware there are other teaching methods that can be used when co-parenting is not a suitable option.

A high conflict divorce leaves many questions, usually unanswered and many situations are left unaddressed.

In theory, mediation and collaborative techniques have promising outcomes; and, for many, they do work. "But" there are always a few parents who just can't pull themselves out, no matter what tools and/or resources are offered. For many such parents, this challenge stems from their own childhood traumas; as child(ren) of divorced parents perhaps; they themselves may have been affected by a "High Conflict" divorce. Parents that also deal with medical challenges such as dealing with stages of bipolar behavior and or other disorders might find they too lack coping skills that throws them into continuous conflict. This brings to light the idea that not all parents CAN co-parent, nor should they try; is a factual statement.

Parallel Parenting gives parents the tools they need to stop the battle, focus on the child(ren), and move on as positive role models, regardless of the other parent's conduct. The results that have been seen from this way of parenting are fewer parents return to court due to missteps by the other parent.

Parallel Parenting is parenting that is not only child(ren) focused, but exclusive of the other parent. There is no direct communication between the parents. Custodial time is carried out as if the other parent no longer existed. The "what if she takes me to court because my kid came home with a broken arm" questions are addressed in practical terms - what if she does take you to court? Did you break your child's arm? If not, what will happen? If you did, that's pretty bad. What do you think the court will do? Maybe you should enroll yourself in anger management before the court orders it. And so on.

Co-parenting is, and always should be, the ultimate goal. Knowing that there are some who physically lack the ability to be a co-parent, yet have the tools and skills to productively parent on their own, will serve the greater, overall interests of the child(ren). Simply said, Parallel Parenting furnishes tools to encourage high conflict parents to be the best parent they can be, regardless of the divorce and regardless of the other parent. It's about learning to be rather than learning to respond.

Since this program deals with Co-Parenting, we are not going to go any further into Parallel Parenting, however the program does exit. Should you be interested, please check your internet for programs in your area.

Chapter 22 - A Healthy Divorce - Financial And Property Issues

Financial and property issues must be decided prior to submitting your paperwork for divorce. These are areas that you and your spouse/partner can mediate to come up with the best situation for you and your family.

Even if you have been married for a short length of time, perhaps both you and your spouse/partner have acquire a fair amount of assets. You owe it to yourself to talk to an attorney, as well as your accountant about your assets and liabilities to come up with a distribution arrangement. Here are some areas that need to be taken care of prior to getting your final divorce decree.

Spousal maintenance and/or alimony,
To sell the house or not,
Division of financial assets: savings, investments, pension and other, retirement plans.
Division of personal property: from pots and pans to furniture and automobiles,
Division of debts: charge accounts, mortgage, loans,
The need for appraisals of property or business interests,
Changing back accounts and credit cards.

HOW TO SPLIT HOUSEHOLD PROPERTY

LOOK AT EACH PIECE OF PERSONAL PROPERTY THAT YOU OWN, DIVIDE UP THE PROPERTY AS FOLLOWS:

DO NOT WANT

Tools

Second Television

Furniture in den

Old dinner plates

Ice maker

Microwave

Refrigerator

HAVE TO HAVE AT ALL COSTS

Stereo

Bedroom set

Living room pictures

Silverware

China

Washer / Dryer

NEGOTIABLE

Television

Dining Set

Couch / Chairs

Hallway pictures

Blender

From the list, you begin to negotiate. Your best end result is to have most of the items in the "Have to have at all cost list", and some of the items in the "Negotiable" list. Good luck!!

WORKBOOK QUESTIONS, INVENTORY HOUSEHOLD ITEMS.

Inventory Notes:

Chapter 23 - A Healthy Divorce - Reminders To Help You Help Your Child(ren) After The Divorce

Do not demean the other parent's living situation, eating habits, choice of friends, choice of activities, choice of dates, or parenting decision. If you have concerns, speak to the other parent personally, far away from the child(ren) hearing.

Help the child(ren) explore their own feelings without influencing them with your own. If positive comments seem impossible, neutral statements about the other parent are better than negative ones.

Do not encourage, in any manner, the child(ren) to be spies or tattlers on the other parent. This can cause a lot of guilty feelings and loyalty conflicts. Assist in dividing the child(ren) things so they will be comfortable in both homes.

Don't let the child(ren) manipulate or play you off against each other. All child(ren) will try this at some point. If there is continuing hostility between parents, the chances for this manipulation to work are greatly improved.

Be honest with your child(ren) but don't burden them with more than they can handle, emotionally or developmentally. Work hard to develop a positive, enthusiastic, optimistic attitude about your custody and access structure. Your attitude will greatly influence your child(ren) attitude.

Do not disappoint your child(ren) by being inconsistent or unpredictable. Stable routine is important. Child(ren) are very hurt if you cancel time with them, show up late to pick them up, or bring them back earlier than planned.

Learn to share your child(ren) comfortably. Give up the need to be intrusive into your former spouse's life or to control what she does with the child(ren). Try to develop trust in her as a parent, even if you have lost trust in her as spouse or friend.

Learn to rebuild your life into one where you are growing in new directions, where you have become happy with yourself, and where you are optimistic about the future. Your sense of well-being and hope will affect your child(ren)'s adjustment in development.

Chapter 24 - A Healthy Divorce - Explore Where You Are, And Where You Are Going After Divorce.

WORKBOOK QUESTIONS,

Find ways for developing new social ties.

Take time to heal emotionally.

Try to understand why your marriage failed.

Be alone with yourself; get to know yourself better before you find a new partner.

Set some new goals and priorities for yourself.

Don't assume that you need to remarry right away.

Build a new social network with people you enjoy.

Consider new educational or career direction.

Take up new sports or civic or religious activities.

Take your time getting into dating or new sexual experiences.

Seek some therapy or support groups if you need help in any of these areas.

Call on parents or other family members for support but don't rely on them exclusively.

Support and protect your child(ren) but don't rely on them to meet your own emotional needs.

Read as much as possible about the effects of divorce on child(ren) and adults.

Learn what you need to know to rebuild a stronger, happier life for yourself and for your child(ren).

(24-1) Once divorced, you might want to take the time to reflect on your marriage, what was good about the relationship, what were some of the factors that contributed to your marriage failing?

_____

_____

_____

_____

(24-2) Are there some specific reasons or issues why you separated and or divorced? If not please describe other factors that perhaps contributed to your separation and or divorce?

_____ Baggage from the families we grew up in,

_____ Baggage from previous relationships,

_____ Stress from being parents,

_____ In-laws,

_____ Child(ren),

_____ Health,

_____ Finances,

_____ Jobs,

_____ Friends,

_____ Loss of interest,

_____ My personal limitations and liabilities,

_____ Anger,

_____ Dependency,

_____ Possessiveness,

_____ Intimacy problems,

_____ Infidelity,

_____ Abuse,

_____ Drug Use /Alcohol Problems,

_____ Other factors _____

(24-3) What do I really want from a committed, long-term relationship?

_____
_____
_____
_____

(24-4) What changes do I need to make to achieve that type of relationship?

_____
_____
_____
_____

(24-5) What type of partner do I need to achieve that type of relationship?

(24-6) What can I do about my personal limitations and liabilities to change them to strengths and resources?

NOTES:

Chapter 25 - A Healthy Divorce - Discover A New Life Within; Setting Long And Short Term Goals

WORKBOOK QUESTIONS,

PROTECT YOURSELF AND YOUR OWN INNER CHILD IN ORDER THAT THE SPIRIT OF LIFE WITHIN YOU MAY FLOURISH.

MY COURSE OF ACTION AS I MOVE FORWARD:

1. _____

2. _____

3. _____

4. _____

5. _____

DEVELOP YOUR TALENTS WITH DEDICATION AND DISCIPLINE, TAKING THEM SERIOUSLY AS THE GIFTS THAT THEY ARE.

MY BEST PERSONAL TRAITS:

_____

_____

_____

MY BEST PROFESSIONAL TRAITS:

_____

_____

_____

_____

MEETING MY NEEDS

Do I need:

_____ More supportive people around me

_____ More education

_____ More money

_____ A good book

_____ A different physical environment

_____ A different routine

_____ More organization

_____ A more specific goal

_____ A creative outlet

_____ Something accomplished

DETERMINE YOUR NEEDS AND MAKE PLANS TO MEET THEM YOURSELF TAKING ACTION EACH DAY.

LONG TERM GOALS:

_____

_____

_____

TOMORROW'S GOALS:

_____

_____

_____

GOALS TO OBTAIN MY SELF WORTH:

MY NEEDS: WHAT DO I NEED TO DO WITHIN MY GOALS TO OBTAIN MY LONG TERM AND TOMORROW'S GOALS?

Example: If your long term goal is to finish college, then you need to do certain things to obtain success within your goal. Without making detailed plans, more than likely, you will not finish your goals. Planning the entire project from start to finish will make you successful. Here is what it could take and what tasks must be finished to be successful, in this case "to finish college." 1. Get a second job to pay for college, 2. Take prerequisites courses, 3. Find a babysitter for evening classes, 4. Apply for scholarship, 5. Enroll in class, 6. Buy school supplies for class.

_____

_____

_____

_____

_____

Build structure into your days and your life. Your inner child feels more secure, for example, when you know you are working out every Monday and Friday as well as doing the laundry on Saturday. Structure and routine is important to bring harmony to your body and mind.

MY THINGS TO DO LIST:

Project Name:/Due Date:/Project Moved To Next Day: / FINISHED

_____

_____

_____

_____

_____

_____

_____

_____

_____

_____

Chapter 26 - A Healthy Divorce - Spousal Abuse, Verbal Abuse, Sexual Abuse, And Physical Abuse

SPOUSE ABUSE IDENTIFICATION QUESTIONNAIRE

PLEASE CHECK THE STATEMENT IF IT PERTAINS TO YOU. SOME QUESTIONS HAVE ADDITIONAL QUESTIONS, YOU MAY WISH TO ANSWER.

Were either you or your spouse physically abused in childhood?

YES _____ NO _____

If so, in what way?

_____

Were either of you emotionally abused during childhood?

YES _____ NO _____

If so, in what way?

_____

Was there a history of violence in either of your families?

YES _____ NO _____

If so, in what way?

_____

If so, was the violence directed at the child(ren), or was it directed at one parent by the other? YES _____ NO _____

If so, in what way?

_____

Does either your spouse or his / her parents abuse alcohol?

YES _____ NO _____

If so, in what way?

_____

Do you? YES _____ NO _____

If so, in what way?

_____

Do your parents? YES _____ NO _____

If so, in what way?
_____

Does your spouse treat his / her parents roughly or disrespectfully?

YES _____ NO _____

Has your spouse ever hit his / her parents, brothers, or sisters?

YES _____ NO _____

Has your spouse ever threatened to harm you? YES _____ NO _____

Are your spouse's problems usually blamed on you or others?

YES _____ NO _____

Have you been attacked or blamed when your spouse got angry?

YES _____ NO _____

Are you afraid of your spouse's temper? YES _____ NO _____

When drinking, does your spouse get rough or violent?

YES _____ NO _____

Has your spouse ever hurt you? When? What happened?

YES _____ NO _____

Did your spouse ever hit a former spouse or lover? YES _____ NO _____

Has your spouse ever deliberately hurt or killed a pet? YES _____ NO _____

Does your spouse have a Dr. Jekyll and Mr. Hyde personality?

YES _____ NO _____

Do you usually give in to settle arguments? YES _____ NO _____

Are your child(ren) afraid when your spouse is angry?

YES _____ NO _____

Have you felt free to invite family or friends to visit you?

YES _____ NO _____

Are you socially active or more socially isolated? YES _____ NO _____

Does your spouse listen in when you're talking on the phone?

YES _____ NO _____

Does your spouse insist on going everywhere with you?

YES _____ NO _____

Is your spouse suspicious of your every move? YES _____ NO _____

Is your spouse an extremely jealous person? YES _____ NO _____

Has your spouse ever forced or pressured you to have sex even though you did not want to? YES _____ NO _____

Have you ever called, or thought of calling, the police because an argument was getting out of control? YES _____ NO _____

Have your neighbors or friends ever called the police because of your situation?

YES _____ NO _____

If the police were called, was your spouse arrested or given a citation?

YES _____ NO _____

Does your spouse ever threaten to take the child(ren) where you could not find them?

YES _____ NO _____

Did this ever occur? YES _____ NO _____

Do you feel safer when we talk with you alone or when you are taking this questionnaire when no one is home or looking over your shoulder?

YES _____ NO _____

AT THE BACK OF THIS PROGRAM YOU WILL FIND A RESOURCE DIRECTORY. PLEASE FEEL FREE TO CONTACT ANY NUMBER THAT YOU FIND IN OUR DIRECTORY.

VERBAL ABUSE OR SPOUSAL ABUSE.

In your own terminology, what is verbal abuse?

_____

_____

_____

Is your spouse verbally abusive? Yes _____ No _____

To whom?

_____

How does it affect the child(ren)?

_____

How does it affect you?

_____

Is it time to say that is enough? Yes _____ No _____

Why now?

_____

SEXUAL OR PHYSICAL ABUSE

In your own terminology, what is sexual or physical abuse?

_____

Is your spouse a child(ren) abuser? Yes _____ No _____

Is he sexually abusive, physically abusive or both?

_____

To whom?

_____

How does it affect the child(ren)?

_____

How does it affect you?

_____

Is it time to say that is enough? Yes _____ No _____

Why now?

_____

Recourse to take:

WE DO RECOMMEND OUTSIDE ASSISTANCE TO WORK WITH YOU AND YOUR FAMILY; AS WELL AS PROTECTION IF NECESSARY. THIS COURSE IS ONLY FOR THE PURPOSE OF IDENTIFYING; PLEASE ASK FOR HELP IF THERE IS A PROBLEM. THIS IS NOT A TREATMENT PROGRAM.

DISCUSSIONS REGARDING CHILD ABUSE.

THERE ARE ALWAYS TWO SIDES TO A STORY, AND TWO OPPOSING PARTIES.

Is child abuse a serious problem? YES _____ NO _____

What causes child abuse?

_____

_____

How can I report child abuse?

_____

_____

Will changes in the criminal justice system help prevent child sexual abuse? YES ____ NO____

Yes: Child Abuse Is a Serious Problem

The Incidence of Child Abuse Is Increasing:

Statistics gathered in a recent national survey indicate that the number of reported incidents of child abuse has increased. In addition, the number of children who were substantiated as victims of abuse has risen as well. Moreover, the same study has indicated that fatalities due to child abuse are vastly underreported.

Child Sexual Abuse Is a Widespread Problem:

The fight against child sexual abuse has often been referred to as a modern day "Salem witch hunt," in which scores of innocent people have been sent to prison on nothing more than the word of a child(ren). The fight against child sexual abuse is not a witch-hunt however the comparison is entirely inaccurate because witches did not exist in seventeenth-century Salem, whereas sexual predators do exist in modem times - in vast numbers.

Child Abuse Fatalities Are Undercounted:

A significant number of children's deaths that have been attributed to sudden infant death syndrome, undetermined cause, or recorded, as accidents are actually the result of abuse or neglect. Medical professionals have found that deaths from child abuse have been underreported by as much as fifty percent, and law enforcement officials seldom conduct thorough investigations into suspicious child(ren)'s deaths. No: Child Abuse is Not a Serious Problem

The Prevalence of Child Abuse is Exaggerated:

Studies that indicate a rising prevalence of child abuse are flawed because many of the child abuse reports in these studies fall into suspect categories, such as "endangered child(ren)." Child(ren) in this category have not actually been abused, but are merely in danger of being abused. By exaggerating the extent of child abuse, child protection experts are actually endangering child(ren) by making the child abuse problem appear too large to solve.

False Allegations of Child Sexual Abuse Are a Serious Problem:

Many innocent people are languishing in prison as a result of the rampant child(ren) sex abuse hysteria of the late 1980s and early 1990s. Scores were convicted simply on the basis of ridiculous allegations that were wrestled from intimidated child(ren) by overly ambitious therapists and prosecutors in poorly conducted trials.

WHAT CAUSES CHILD ABUSE?

Substance Abuse Is Responsible For Child Abuse

Parents who abuse drugs or alcohol are almost three times more likely to physically or sexually assault their child(ren) than are other parents. The rate of neglect for child(ren) of substance-abusing parents is more than four times the rate of neglect for child(ren) of non-substance-abusing parents.

Family Preservation Laws Put Child(Ren) At Risk For Abuse

The press has portrayed many recent child(ren) abuse fatalities as the result of oversights by overworked, understaffed, and under-funded child(ren) welfare agencies, whose workers let at-risk child(ren) "slip through the cracks." In reality, half of the 1,500 children who die as a result of abuse each year are already known to the child(ren) welfare system. These children are victims of a family preservation policy that consistently reunited vulnerable children with abusive parents who cannot be rehabilitated.

The Foster Care System Exposes Child(Ren) To Abuse

The idea that a child(ren) is safe when he or she is taken away from an abusive or neglectful parent and placed in foster care is a myth. Research has determined that child(ren) in foster care are twice as likely to be abused as child(ren) who live with their natural parents.

Parental Cohabitation Exposes Child(Ren) Greater Risk Of Abuse

Many recent child abuse fatalities are the direct result of society's loosening of the taboo against cohabitation. Though other factors contribute to a child(ren)'s risk of being abuse, studies have consistently shown that the presence of an unrelated man in the home greatly increases the chance that the child(ren) will be assaulted.

Poverty Cause's Child Abuse

Every national survey of child abuse and neglect has indicated that the majority of such incidents involved families from the lowest socioeconomic levels. Research has indicated that the problems of poverty - unemployment, substandard housing, insufficient money, food, and recreation - cause the stressful situations that can precipitate child abuse and neglect.

Chapter 27 - A Healthy Divorce - A Discussion Regarding When Parents Kidnap

A DISCUSSION ABOUT WHEN PARENTS KIDNAP

Several studies have been done on profiles of an abductor. One study showed Caucasian parents were more likely to abduct and more likely to be male than female. Single abductions were more common than those involving multiple children and victims were equally likely to be male or female. Abductors tend to have previous criminal records. Child(ren) who were abducted for shorter periods of time were apt to experience fewer traumas. Another study concluded international kidnapping accounted for 18% of the study, again men left the country more than women.

Domestic abductions were resolved more often than kids taken internationally. Parents left behind generally believed law-enforcement agencies were less interested in helping them, than in helping parents whose child(ren) were taken by strangers. The searching parent spent from $10,000 up to excess of $50,000 to find their child(ren).

Other studies showed fathers abducted more prior to custody having been established and mothers abducted after custody was established. Range of time for child(ren) missing was from 4 hours to 13 years. In this particular study, revenge was a consistent theme. Other reasons for abductions included the abductor's desire to be noticed or persuaded which was seen as a replay of the couples courtship dance. Some ran because of accusations of sexual and/or physical abuse, as well as mental breakdowns and emotional problems.

Stranger abduction is rare compared to parent abduction. Physical and sexual abuse during abduction is unusual affecting less than 5% of child(ren). One out of six children was seriously mentally harmed by the abduction. Security word holidays note word and page number. Half of the abductions lasted less than one week. Many parents knew where their child(ren) were during their abduction. In this study only a handful of kids were still missing. Studies are just that; studies.

Very few people need to be aware or worried that situations like this could happen to their family.

AS ALWAYS:

You need to keep the communication lines open.

Your job is not to punish, condemn, but to compromise and find the best solution for your family.

If your spouse threatens to take your child(ren), take the threat seriously. Report the threat to authorities. If you have an attorney, do whatever is necessary to protect your child(ren).

A healthy divorce is the best solution to offset this result.

MOVIES/ REFERENCE

Video #1 Dysfunctional Family

Video #2 Importance of Play

National and Local Resources for Inquiries and Help Line

REMEMBER ABUSE IS NOT "ALWAYS" PHYSICAL

ABUSE RESOURCES

National Domestic Violence Hotline 1-800-799-SAFE(7233)

Florida Department of Children and Families: Florida Abuse Hotline

Department of Justice: Defending Childhood

Department of Justice: Office on Violence Against Women

National Child Abuse Hotline 1-800-4-A-CHILD(422-4453)

National Coalition Against Domestic Violence 303-839-1852

National Network to End Domestic Violence 202-543-5566

Rape, Abuse & Incest National Network

National Sexual Violence Resource Center 877-739-3895

The National Center for Victims of Crime 202-467-8700

COMMUNITY RESOURCES

Emergency Services / Dial 9-1-1

National Association of Social Workers

United Way (Dial 2-1-1 Referral Resources)

COLLABORATIVE ONLINE CALENDARS

OurFamilyWizard.com

Cozi.com

Google Calendar

KeepandShare.com

LEGAL RESOURCES

American Academy of Matrimonial Lawyers 321-263-6477

FindLaw: Divorce Information & Attorney Directory

Legal Services Corporation: Legal Aid Directory 202-295-1500

MENTAL HEALTH RESOURCES

American Mental Health Counselors Association 800-326-2642

American Psychiatric Association 703-907-7300

Substance Abuse and Mental Health Services Administration

SUBSTANCE ABUSE RESOURCES

Alcoholics Anonymous 212-870-340 Narcotics Anonymous

National Institute on Drug Abuse 301-443-1124

Substance Abuse and Mental Health Services Administration

Parental Alienation Awareness Organization USA

National Parent Helpline 855-4-A-PARENT (427-2736)

US DEPT OF HEALTH & HUMAN SERVICES

Parent Support Group Resources

Parent Support Group Programs

Administration for Children & Families

The Office of Child Support Enforcement

US DEPT OF JUSTICE

Defending Childhood

American Academy of Pediatrics

GREAT NEWS! Our program "A Healthy Divorce" gives you all the tools that are required by state courts to fill out your PARENTING PLANS. The following are instructions and an example of a Parenting Plan, in this case used in Florida. We have used Florida as an "example" of what is needed when filling out a detailed plan. Florida allows this form or similar forms be used in final proceedings. Perhaps your state has the same or similar laws/forms.

Please check with your state to see if you can use this form or perhaps your state requires you use a specific form generated by your state agencies. This course is for educational purposes only and cannot advise you on individual states administrative rules. Each state has different rules and procedures. You will want to follow your state's laws and administrative procedures as you prepare your Parenting Plan. Most important, feel confident after finishing this course; you are extremely prepared and should feel well versed regarding how to prepare for your divorce and parenting plan. Thank you.

[Florida Supreme Court Approved Family Law Form 12.995(A), Parenting Plan http://www.flcourts.org/core/fileparse.php/293/urlt/995a.pdf](http://www.flcourts.org/core/fileparse.php/293/urlt/995a.pdf)

[Florida Supreme Court Approved Family Law Form 12.995(B), Supervised/Safety-Focused Parenting Plan http://www.flcourts.org/core/fileparse.php/293/urlt/995b.pdf](http://www.flcourts.org/core/fileparse.php/293/urlt/995b.pdf)

[Florida Supreme Court Approved Family Law Form 12.995(C), Relocation/Long Distance Parenting Plan http://flcourts.org/core/fileparse.php/293/urlt/995c.pdf](http://flcourts.org/core/fileparse.php/293/urlt/995c.pdf)

Going Pro Se?
(Representing Yourself)?
What that tells us, is you have a lot of courage.
Going it alone is complicated.

AS YOUR MEDIATOR, WE PROMISE YOU:
Mediating your case does not cost a lot of money.
Think about using a Mediator when filing your papers and negotiating your divorce.

We can help you through all of your critical decision making choices.
Decisions that will affect your life as well as your child's development and care.

Major decisions like child custody, child support, and visitation along with a parenting plan can be resolved.
Financial planning including investments, your home, and other properties can be resolved without using attorneys.

Think Mediation when you start your Divorce Negotiations.

SOME COUNTIES PROVIDE MEDIATION, HOWEVER YOU ARE NOT ALLOWED TO MEDIATE SOME ISSUES THAT YOU MAY FIND IMPORTANT.

Should you decide to go court ordered mediation, (THROUGH THE COURT) here are the facts. First you are only allowed to mediate just a few items. The rest of the divorce will be handled by the courts and all items will be decided by your judge.
Issues that are important to you!

Don't leave your future, your finances, and your family's life to a process where the court can make final decisions regarding the care and the well-being of your family.
Leaving your case to a judge's determination could end with a final order or decision that you simply don't want. Please consider mediation, for the sake of your family, for the sake of your future.

MEDIATION DOES WORK. WE CAN FIND A MEDIATOR IN YOUR TOWN THAT IS RIGHT FOR YOU.
Why not give us a call today. We are here to assist you.
Let's have a conversation.

DEBORAH SHOOTER
PHONE: 407-324-2400

THE BEST SOLUTION TO RESOLVING YOUR DIVORCE

Test Questions

THE TEST CONSISTS OF 10 TRUE AND FALSE QUESTIONS. YOU MAY MISS TWO QUESTIONS AND STILL PASS. IF YOU MISS MORE THAN TWO QUESTIONS, YOUR INSTRUCTOR WILL ADVISE YOU ON WHAT THEIR COMPANY POLICY IS FOR RETAKING THE TEST.

1. Working together for the betterment of the child(ren) helps the child(ren) to develop and gives them better access to both parents. Equal rights and shared parenting, does not always mean that both parents get access to their child(ren) 50% (equally) all of the time.
_____ TRUE _____ FALSE

2. All people, when they have fantasies react and act out to what they fantasized about.
_____ TRUE _____ FALSE

3. In the grieving process, you are still holding onto the hope that your marriage will be restored. There is a willingness to change anything about yourself. You are willing to do anything; if you could just get it right, your spouse would return. The important thing to learn during this stage is that you can't control the thoughts, desires or actions of another human being. This is the Bargaining Stage.
_____ TRUE _____ FALSE

4. Grandparents are not important in your child's development. Child(ren) should only have access to all their grandparents and other extended family members during holidays.
_____ TRUE _____ FALSE

5. Be honest with your child(ren) about the reasons for the decision to separate, but refrain from blaming, criticizing, or exaggerating.
_____ TRUE _____ FALSE

6. Make sure the school has both parent's emergency information and permission for both parents (if allowed by the courts) to pick up their child(ren). Both parents in most cases should be allowed access to all school records.

_____ TRUE _____ FALSE

7. Child support guidelines consider: The income of both parents, the child(ren)'s health care and child care costs, and the standard needs for the child(ren). A list of support amounts based on the child(ren)'s age and net income of the parents is in the Florida law/standard needs table.

_____ TRUE _____ FALSE

8. In today's world communication between families is not important. After divorce it is better for parents to do what they want with the children when it is their turn to have visitation.

_____ TRUE _____ FALSE

9. "If my spouse wants to see the kids then he/she can come and pick them up and bring them back. It is not my job to transport the children." This is a good co-parenting skill.

_____ TRUE _____ FALSE

10. A good co-parent starts with me.

_____ TRUE _____ FALSE

CPSIA information can be obtained
at www.ICGtesting.com
Printed in the USA
FSOW04n0218220217
30990FS